THE DOLPHINS AT
50

LEGENDS AND MEMORIES FROM SOUTH FLORIDA'S MOST CELEBRATED TEAM

BY THE STAFF OF THE
SunSentinel

WITH A FOREWORD BY JASON TAYLOR // INTRODUCTION BY DAVE HYDE

TRIUMPH
BOOKS

This book is available in quantity at special discounts for your group or organization. For further information, contact:

Triumph Books LLC
814 North Franklin Street
Chicago, Illinois 60610
Phone: (312) 337-0747
www.triumphbooks.com

Printed in U.S.A.
ISBN: 978-1-62937-178-8

EDITORS: Kathy Laughlin, Keven Lerner

DESIGNERS: David Schutz, Bill Passonno

PHOTOGRAPHY EDITOR: George Wilson

CONTRIBUTORS: Dave Hyde, Steve Svekis, Omar Kelly, Chris Perkins, Steve McGrath, David Baker and Michael Cumella

Dolphins defensive end Bill Stanfill puts pressure on Steelers QB Terry Bradshaw in a 1971 game.

THE DOLPHINS AT

50

LEGENDS AND MEMORIES
FROM SOUTH FLORIDA'S
MOST CELEBRATED TEAM

TABLE OF CONTENTS

Dolphins logo
1966-73

1

THE TRADITION

FOREWORD

JASON TAYLOR

**NO. 99 LOOKS BACK ON HIS UNEXPECTED
JOURNEY TO MIAMI AND HOW HIS COACHES
AND TEAMMATES – AND THE DOLPHINS COMMUNITY –
SHAPED HIS LIFE AND CAREER.**

{ AS TOLD TO DAVE HYDE }

When I think about it now, it's funny how everything changed in my mom's Pittsburgh home that Saturday in 1997. I didn't want a draft party, but mom did, and so I sat anxiously among family and friends to see where my football future led. Would Tennessee take me, as rumored? My hometown Steelers, as hoped?

Somewhere in the third round, the phone rang and the voice at the other end said, "Hey, Jason, this is Jimmy Johnson of the Miami Dolphins … ."

So my football path started with a team I knew casually from being a fan of Dan Marino, another Pittsburgh guy who I grew up watching. Now he was my teammate. And soon my friend. He also in time became a bridge for me to the great history of the Dolphins, since he played with Hall of Famers like Don Shula and Dwight Stephenson, who in turn played with members of the legendary teams of the 1970s.

One thing you learned quickly with the Dolphins was tradition mattered and the great names endured. I met them all through the years — Larry Csonka, Larry Little, Paul Warfield, Bob Griese and on down the line. I enjoyed being part of a franchise with deep roots of success. It set a standard for us to try to meet. When my name was added to the Dolphins' Honor Roll, that carried significance in part because of the group I was joining.

Of course, I was a skinny young kid upon arriving to the Dolphins. In fact, I was so skinny that for the first three years in the league I'd eat peanut-butter-and-jelly sandwiches as fast as they could be made and drank bottles of water before team weigh-ins just to appear a few pounds heavier than I was.

It wasn't until midway through a struggling third season that I took the advice of veteran teammate Trace Armstrong: Be yourself. That was it. That's when I turned the corner, too. I quit trying to gain weight and become a prototypical, 275-pound defensive end. I played around 240 pounds. I tried to be the best version of myself. I went from doubting myself to being dumbfounded I was good enough as I was. That's the advice I have for players today — and for students who will never play pro football. Be yourself. Trust that's good enough. That's what I learned.

I had plenty of help from those around me, too. My teammates, of course. Jimmy taught me to be a pro. Nick Saban arrived and changed my entire role in a manner that worried me. Instead of playing as a normal hand-in-the-dirt defensive end, I moved all over the defense. I remember talking to Nick about that role and his philosophies on the phone for 45 minutes while driving a boat to the Keys. In that new role, I was the NFL's Defensive Player of the Year in 2006. So another lesson was learned. Don't fear change. Embrace smart change.

As my career went on, everything changed. I met my wife. We started a family. We also worked to become part of the community. For years, I went to players' charities in the offseason to watch how they ran events. I watched Marino, again, in his work with autism. I didn't just want to have a great career. I wanted to impact my community. I knew what it was like to grow up poor and without direction. I loved when an athlete came to talk at an event. So it's important, years after my career is over, that The Jason Taylor Foundation is helping students find their path through staples such as after-school programs and creative ideas like poetry contests.

I was lucky. I knew my path from Jimmy Johnson's phone call. It wasn't always easy. But anyone who wore a Dolphins jersey in the franchise's 50 seasons knows, like I do, what a blessing it's been.

INTRODUCTION

DAVE HYDE

{ SUN SENTINEL SPORTS COLUMNIST }

 The Miami Dolphins were born in the manner sports teams never are anymore: With no money. Joe Robbie was a Minneapolis lawyer with seven children who never earned more than $27,000 a year. Danny Thomas was a renowned actor who capped his investment at $25,000. When newly named AFL Commissioner Al Davis saw the Dolphins' financial books after the franchise started in 1966, he said, "We've got a problem."

Fifty years later, they have an iconic franchise. Robbie's rags-to-riches dream came true. The Dolphins' portfolio is rich and varied: The league's only Perfect Season in 1972; two Super Bowl titles and five Super Bowl appearances; nine Hall of Famers and pro football's all-time winningest coach in Don Shula.

As much as anything in South Florida, the Dolphins came to define the region for their first few decades in a manner only the best sports team do. South Florida was considered a sleepy retirement home and spring break haven when the Dolphins arrived in 1966. They gave it a national definition within the great Dolphins teams of the early-1970s and had the highest winning percentage among American sports teams for the first few decades of play.

When Dan Marino arrived in 1983, the Dolphins under Shula and Robbie added an electric talent to usher in a new generation of winning and fans. Robbie continued his gambling ways when Miami commissioners refused to build a publicly funded stadium. He built one with private money. Joe Robbie Stadium opened in 1987, a new vista into a richer sports culture, as shown by the franchise's worth. Robbie paid a $7.5 million franchise fee to start the team. After he died in 1990, H. Wayne Huizenga became a part owner of the team and stadium, and in 1994 became the sole owner of both. By 2009, Steve Ross had taken over 95% ownership of the team and stadium in exchange for about $1.1 billion total.

If success has waned in the new millennium and attention has wandered in a grown-up South Florida sports scene, the Dolphins remain the region's anchor as its founding franchise. Ross was a season-ticket holder during the great teams in the 1970s. He now sits in the owner's box. "This is the fans' team; I'm just holding it for a while," he said.

Joe Robbie

H. Wayne
Huizenga

Steve Ross

11

Dolphins logo
1974-89

2
THE SEASONS

SEASON RECORDS

AFTER 49 YEARS, THE DOLPHINS HAVE A WINNING RECORD, A PERFECT SEASON AND TWO SUPER BOWL TITLES. A LOOK BACK AT EVERY DOLPHINS SEASON.

423
REGULAR-SEASON WINS

325
REGULAR-SEASON LOSSES

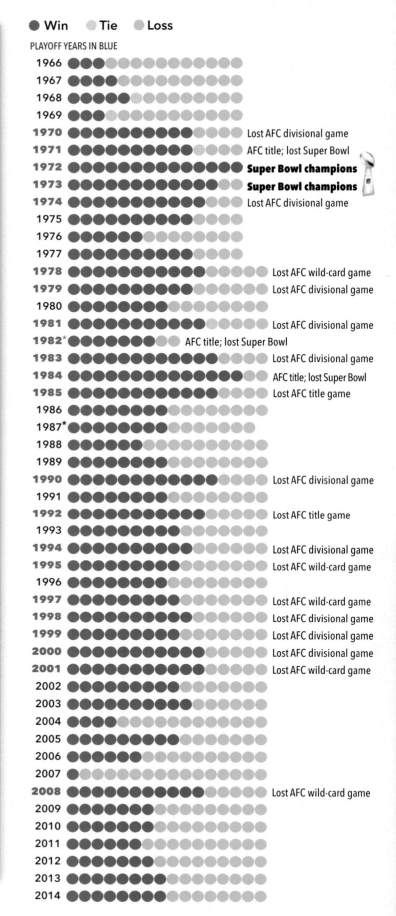

● Win ● Tie ● Loss

PLAYOFF YEARS IN BLUE

1966	
1967	
1968	
1969	
1970	Lost AFC divisional game
1971	AFC title; lost Super Bowl
1972	**Super Bowl champions**
1973	**Super Bowl champions**
1974	Lost AFC divisional game
1975	
1976	
1977	
1978	Lost AFC wild-card game
1979	Lost AFC divisional game
1980	
1981	Lost AFC divisional game
1982*	AFC title; lost Super Bowl
1983	Lost AFC divisional game
1984	AFC title; lost Super Bowl
1985	Lost AFC title game
1986	
1987*	
1988	
1989	
1990	Lost AFC divisional game
1991	
1992	Lost AFC title game
1993	
1994	Lost AFC divisional game
1995	Lost AFC wild-card game
1996	
1997	Lost AFC wild-card game
1998	Lost AFC divisional game
1999	Lost AFC divisional game
2000	Lost AFC divisional game
2001	Lost AFC wild-card game
2002	
2003	
2004	
2005	
2006	
2007	
2008	Lost AFC wild-card game
2009	
2010	
2011	
2012	
2013	
2014	

* Shortened season due to NFL players strike

Coach Don Shula gets a victory shower from his players after notching his 300th NFL win on Sept. 22, 1991.

1966

REGULAR SEASON: WON 3, LOST 11
Finished fourth (tied) in AFL East
HEAD COACH: George Wilson

Joe Auer returned the opening kickoff in Miami Dolphins history 95 yards for a touchdown in a 23-14 loss to the Oakland Raiders in the Orange Bowl.

Joe Auer scored two second-half touchdowns, and Dolphins quarterback George Wilson Jr. averaged 19.6 yards per completion as Miami handled the Denver Broncos 24-7 in the Orange Bowl on Oct. 16 for the franchise's first win.

The Dolphins won their first road game and created their first win streak in one fell swoop as Miami toppled the Houston Oilers 20-13 the week after the Broncos win. Wilson completed his first four passes — including an 80-yard TD to Bo Roberson — before exiting the game with an injury, and the Dolphins went wire-to-wire at Rice Stadium, where, 7 1/2 years later, they would win their most recent NFL title.

Sept. 2	OAKLAND	L	14-23
Sept. 9	NEW YORK JETS	L	14-19
Sept. 18	at Buffalo	L	24-58
Oct. 2	at San Diego	L	10-44
Oct. 9	at Oakland	L	10-21
Oct. 16	**DENVER**	**W**	**24-7**
Oct. 23	**at Houston**	**W**	**20-13**
Nov. 6	BUFFALO	L	0-29
Nov. 13	at Kansas City	L	16-34
Nov. 20	at New York Jets	L	13-30
Nov. 27	BOSTON	L	14-20
Dec. 4	at Denver	L	7-17
Dec. 11	KANSAS CITY	L	18-19
Dec. 18	**HOUSTON**	**W**	**29-28**

◄ George Wilson, the Dolphins' first head coach, sees his team losing to the Jets in 1969. He went 15-39-2 as Miami's coach.

1967

REGULAR SEASON: WON 4, LOST 10
Finished third (tied) in AFL East
HEAD COACH: George Wilson

Purdue QB Bob Griese was taken with the No. 4 pick in the draft and led the Dolphins to a season-opening 35-21 win over the Denver Broncos with two touchdown passes in his debut.

CB Dick Westmoreland hauled in 10 interceptions, including an amazing seven between Nov. 19 and Dec. 17, during which the Dolphins won three-fourths of their games that season.

Running backs Jack Harper and Stan Mitchell each scored four touchdowns to lead the team. That ties with the 1976 team (which had five such players) as the fewest touchdowns scored by the Dolphins' season leader.

Sept. 17	DENVER	W	35-21
Sept. 24	KANSAS CITY	L	0-24
Oct. 1	at New York Jets	L	7-29
Oct. 8	at Kansas City	L	0-41
Oct. 15	at Boston	L	10-41
Oct. 22	NEW YORK JETS	L	14-33
Nov. 5	at Buffalo	L	13-35
Nov. 12	at San Diego	L	0-24
Nov. 19	at Oakland	L	17-31
Nov. 26	**BUFFALO**	**W**	**17-14**
Dec. 3	at Houston	L	14-17
Dec. 10	**SAN DIEGO**	**W**	**41-24**
Dec. 17	**BOSTON**	**W**	**41-32**
Dec. 23	HOUSTON	L	10-41

◄ Rookie quarterback Bob Griese is tackled by a Buffalo Bills defender in 1967.

1968

REGULAR SEASON: WON 5, LOST 8, TIED 1
Finished third in AFC East
HEAD COACH: George Wilson

The Dolphins drafted Butch and Sundance, also known as running backs Larry Csonka and Jim Kiick. The bruising Csonka out of Syracuse was picked at No. 8, but Wyoming's Kiick didn't get selected until the fifth round.

Receiver Karl Noonan had an amazing season, with 11 touchdown catches in the team's 14 games, seven in the seven road games.

For the only time in club history, the Dolphins played the season's first three games at home. They lost all three.

Sept. 14	HOUSTON	L	10-24
Sept. 21	OAKLAND	L	21-47
Sept. 28	KANSAS CITY	L	3-48
Oct. 6	**at Houston**	**W**	**24-7**
Oct. 12	BUFFALO	T	14-14
Oct. 20	**at Cincinnati**	**W**	**24-22**
Oct. 27	at Denver	L	14-21
Nov. 3	at San Diego	L	28-34
Nov. 10	**at Buffalo**	**W**	**21-17**
Nov. 17	CINCINNATI	L	21-38
Nov. 24	**at Boston**	**W**	**34-10**
Dec. 1	at New York Jets	L	17-35
Dec. 8	**BOSTON**	**W**	**38-7**
Dec. 15	NEW YORK JETS	L	7-31

1969

REGULAR SEASON: WON 3, LOST 10, TIED 1
Finished fifth in AFC East
HEAD COACH: George Wilson

The offseason featured two of the biggest trades in Dolphins history. Miami acquired two future Hall of Famers: linebacker Nick Buoniconti in March from the Boston Patriots and guard Larry Little in July from the San Diego Chargers. Also, the Dolphins drafted future standouts DE Bill Stanfill and RB Mercury Morris.

Quarterback Bob Griese suffered through the worst season of his career, with 10 touchdown passes and 16 interceptions and an atrocious passer rating of 56.9.

The people of Boston wanted no part of watching football games involving the Miami Dolphins in the 1960s. In three visits to Alumni Stadium from 1967-69, the Dolphins drew a combined 42,170 fans. The three games (17,859 fans in 1967, 13,646 in 1968 and 10,665 in 1969) are the three worst-attended Dolphins games in history.

Sept. 14	at Cincinnati	L	21-27
Sept. 20	at Oakland	L	17-20
Sept. 28	at Houston	L	10-22
Oct. 4	OAKLAND	T	20-20
Oct. 11	SAN DIEGO	L	14-21
Oct. 19	at Kansas City	L	10-17
Oct. 26	**BUFFALO**	**W**	**24-6**
Nov. 2	at New York Jets	L	31-34
Nov. 9	**at Boston**	**W**	**17-16**
Nov. 16	at Buffalo	L	3-28
Nov. 23	HOUSTON	L	7-32
Nov. 30	Boston (at Tampa)	L	23-38
Dec. 7	**DENVER**	**W**	**27-24**
Dec. 14	NEW YORK JETS	L	9-27

1970

Dolphins running back Jim Kiick makes a one-handed catch for a first down against the Baltimore Colts on Nov. 22, 1970.

REGULAR SEASON: WON 10, LOST 4
Finished second in AFC East
HEAD COACH: Don Shula

Owner Joe Robbie continued his mastery of the offseason as he acquired wide receiver Paul Warfield from Cleveland and then shipped a first-round pick to the Baltimore Colts to get his coach: Don Shula.

Shula's first Dolphins draft choice was a free-spirited tight end from Michigan and future all-time fan favorite Jim Mandich. After his playing days, Mandich's broadcast career included his signature "Allriiiiiiiight, Miami!" cheers after touchdowns.

RBs Larry Csonka and Jim Kiick combined for 2,123 total yards and 12 rushing touchdowns as the Dolphins made their first playoff appearance, losing 21-14 to the Oakland Raiders.

Sept. 20	at Boston	L	14-27
Sept. 27	at Houston	W	20-10
Oct. 3	OAKLAND	W	20-13
Oct. 10	at New York Jets	W	20-6
Oct. 18	at Buffalo	W	33-14
Oct. 25	CLEVELAND	L	0-28
Nov. 1	at Baltimore	L	0-35
Nov. 8	at Philadelphia	L	17-24
Nov. 15	NEW ORLEANS	W	21-10
Nov. 22	BALTIMORE	W	34-17
Nov. 30	at Atlanta	W	20-7
Dec. 6	BOSTON	W	37-20
Dec. 13	NEW YORK JETS	W	16-10
Dec. 20	BUFFALO	W	45-7

AFC DIVISIONAL PLAYOFF

Dec. 27	at Oakland	L	14-21

Coach Don Shula, center, talks strategy with quarterback Bob Griese and receiver Paul Warfield during a 1970 game.

1971

REGULAR SEASON: WON 10, LOST 3, TIED 1
Finished first in AFC East
HEAD COACH: Don Shula

QB Bob Griese had his best season, the only one in which his touchdown passes exceeded his interceptions by double-digits (19 to 9), as he finished with a 90.9 passer rating, second-best in the NFL.

In the Dolphins' first postseason win they rallied three times to tie the Kansas City Chiefs, and a 5-yard touchdown pass with 1:36 left sent the game to overtime. Garo Yepremian won it with a 37-yard field goal with 7:40 elapsed in the second overtime in the longest game in NFL history (82 minutes, 40 seconds).

A 21-0 AFC Championship rout of the Baltimore Colts sent the Dolphins to New Orleans for Super Bowl VI. They were overmatched against the Dallas Cowboys, losing 24-3. A winding 29-yard sack of Bob Griese by Bob Lilly was the most enduring memory.

Sept. 19	at Denver	T	10-10
Sept. 26	**at Buffalo**	**W**	**29-14**
Oct. 3	NEW YORK JETS	L	10-14
Oct. 10	**at Cincinnati**	**W**	**23-13**
Oct. 17	**NEW ENGLAND**	**W**	**41-3**
Oct. 24	**at New York Jets**	**W**	**30-14**
Oct. 31	**at Los Angeles**	**W**	**20-14**
Nov. 7	**BUFFALO**	**W**	**34-0**
Nov. 14	**PITTSBURGH**	**W**	**24-21**
Nov. 21	**BALTIMORE**	**W**	**17-14**
Nov. 29	**CHICAGO**	**W**	**34-3**
Dec. 5	at New England	L	13-34
Dec. 11	at Baltimore	L	3-14
Dec. 19	**GREEN BAY**	**W**	**27-6**

AFC DIVISIONAL PLAYOFF

Dec. 25	at Kansas City	W 27-24 (2 OT)

AFC CHAMPIONSHIP

Jan 2, 1972	BALTIMORE	W	21-0

SUPER BOWL VI (IN NEW ORLEANS)

Jan. 16	Dallas	L	3-24

The Dolphins rush Cowboys quarterback Roger Staubach as he throws to tight end Mike Ditka, right, in the 1972 Super Bowl.

Far left, Cowboys QB Roger Staubach scrambles against the Dolphins' defense in Super Bowl VI in 1972.

At left, Dolphins defensive linemen Bill Stanfill (84) and Manny Fernandez (75) converge on a Patriots player in 1971.

Tight end Jim Mandich (88) rejoices after Miami scores a TD against the Redskins in Super Bowl VII in 1973. The Dolphins won 14-7 to cap their perfect season.

1972
THE PERFECT SEASON

BY BOB KUECHENBERG
{ DOLPHINS GUARD // 1970-84 }

I always like when an NFL team begins the season with 10 straight wins. People start debating if it can go undefeated. The media starts calling. The possibility of another team matching our 1972 Perfect Season comes into view, and we get to re-live our accomplishment all over again.

But the truth is we never intended to go undefeated that season. It wasn't a private goal, a public thought or even a topic of conversation other than how Jim Langer and I approached it during one of our regular workouts in the team's weight room, if you want to call it that.

The weight room actually was a women's bathroom off the pool at Biscayne College, where the Dolphins facilities were. A Universal gym was placed there. Space was so tight we'd have to put our feet on the wall to do the bench press. Few players noticed, because few actually trained with weights in 1972. But Langer and I did, and somewhere in our workouts each week our growing string of victories would come up.

"When we going to lose, Jim?" I'd say.

"Not this week against the Jets," he'd say.

Or the Bills. Or Patriots. Or whoever became the next week's opponent. At some point, going undefeated came on our radar, just for the reason we couldn't see anyone beating us. But our sole mission that season was to return to the Super Bowl and win it this time, because we'd been embar-

rassed in it the year before by the Dallas Cowboys.

For most teams and many coaches, reaching the Super Bowl would have been an achievement to celebrate, no matter the result. Not for this team. Certainly not for this coach. When we arrived for training camp in 1972, Don Shula was in one word – his word – "obsessed" about avenging that loss and winning the Super Bowl. And, like any great leader, his mindset became our mindset as players as well.

That worked just fine for us, because we were a motivated bunch to begin with. Just look at the offensive line I played guard on. We were all rejects. Norm Evans was cast away by Houston in the 1966 expansion draft. Larry Little was traded from San Diego for little-regarded cornerback Mack Lamb, who just happened to be Little's high school teammate. San Francisco tried to smuggle Wayne Moore through the waiver wire by using his real first name, Solomon, which was recognized by our great offensive line coach, Monte Clark. Cleveland put Langer on waivers, and Clark, who had played in Cleveland, grabbed him on a former teammate's recommendation.

Me? I came to the Dolphins from selling business forms during the week and playing for the semi-pro Chicago Owls on the weekend. I'd been a fourth-round pick of Philadelphia who lost the love of football and left their training camp. But somewhere between playing football with the Owls, having postgame beer and pizza and watching guys I was better than playing in the NFL renewed my motivation. I went down the NFL roster to see which teams were desperate for guards.

That's how I became a Dolphin, and by the third game of 1972 lined up against Minnesota's great defense, the Purple People Eaters of Alan Page and Carl Eller. That was our closest call that season. On the road. On grass (we were a better artificial-turf team). On the wrong side of the scoreboard with five minutes left. Garo Yepremian then made a 51-yard field goal, the longest of his career to that point, to cut Minnesota's lead to five points. Bob Griese then called a pass on first-and-goal when everyone expected a handoff to Larry Csonka. Jim Mandich caught the victory touchdown.

That was the only game we didn't control all season. You might say we only beat the Bills 24-23, but they scored late to make it look close. There was the first playoff game where we trailed late. We ran the running play — that "36 Trap" — that was a staple of our offense. Jim Kiick read my block, ran 12 yards for a touchdown, and we were off to beat Pitts-

Don Shula wears a smile as his team pummels the Patriots 52-0 on Nov. 12, 1972, to improve to 9-0.

burgh for the AFC Championship.

The Super Bowl against Washington went almost according to script. Our offense punished Washington. And our No-Name Defense, as they were called? Defensive tackle Manny Fernandez had 17 tackles, safety Jake Scott had two interceptions and middle linebacker Nick Buoniconti did what he did every Sunday, which was outsmart the quarterback throughout the game.

It was 14-0 when Yepremian went to line up a 42-yard field goal in the fourth quarter. Dolphins owner Joe Robbie sent word to the press box the field goal would make it a symmetrical 17-0 score in a 17-0 season. The attempt was botched, the Redskins got a touchdown, but we still got exactly what we wanted out of that day.

"17-0," it says on our rings. You don't need to say more than that. But I did years later on my business letterhead to underscore the achievement of that year: "Perfection is immortal; imperfection is … just that."

{ AS TOLD TO DAVE HYDE }

◀ Former coach Don Shula, center in jacket, and the Dolphins team he led to an undefeated season in 1972 wave to the crowd during a 2007 halftime ceremony. Shown with Shula are, from left, Larry Csonka, Jim Langer, Larry Little, Mercury Morris, Nick Buoniconti and Lloyd Mumphord.

1972

REGULAR SEASON: WON 14, LOST 0
Finished first in AFC East
HEAD COACH: Don Shula

Sept. 17	at Kansas City	W	20-10
Sept. 24	HOUSTON	W	34-13
Oct. 1	at Minnesota	W	16-14
Oct. 8	at New York Jets	W	27-17
Oct. 15	SAN DIEGO	W	24-10
Oct. 22	BUFFALO	W	24-23
Oct. 29	at Baltimore	W	23-0
Nov. 5	at Buffalo	W	30-16
Nov. 12	NEW ENGLAND	W	52-0
Nov. 19	NEW YORK JETS	W	28-24
Nov. 27	ST. LOUIS	W	31-10
Dec. 3	at New England	W	37-21
Dec. 10	at New York Giants	W	23-13
Dec. 16	BALTIMORE	W	16-0

AFC DIVISIONAL PLAYOFF

Dec. 24	CLEVELAND	W	20-14

AFC CHAMPIONSHIP

Dec. 31	at Pittsburgh	W	21-17

SUPER BOWL VII (IN LOS ANGELES)

Jan. 14, 1973	Washington	W	14-7

◀ In the fifth week of the season, starting QB Bob Griese, right, fractured his ankle. Coach Don Shula, center, had to send in the backup, 38-year-old Earl Morrall, left. Morrall started nine games and kept the Dolphins undefeated until Griese returned two months later.

Coach Don Shula is carried off the field after the Dolphins won Super Bowl VII in Los Angeles to complete their 17-0 season.

1973

REGULAR SEASON: WON 12, LOST 2
Finished first in AFC East
HEAD COACH: Don Shula

While the previous year's squad earned immortality, the 1973 edition put on the most dominant postseason in Dolphins history, winning all three playoff games by at least 17 points, capped off by the 24-7 decimation of a talent-laden Minnesota Vikings team in Super Bowl VIII in Houston.

On Sept. 30, Mercury Morris scored three TDs and set a franchise record for rushing yards in a game with 197 on 15 carries in a victory over the New England Patriots. The record stood until 2002.

From Nov. 4 through Nov. 22, the Dolphins strung together a franchise-record 13 consecutive quarters without allowing a point.

Sept. 16	SAN FRANCISCO	W	21-13
Sept. 23	at Oakland	L	7-12
Sept. 30	NEW ENGLAND	W	44-23
Oct. 7	NEW YORK JETS	W	31-3
Oct. 15	at Cleveland	W	17-9
Oct. 21	BUFFALO	W	27-6
Oct. 28	at New England	W	30-14
Nov. 4	at New York Jets	W	24-14
Nov. 11	BALTIMORE	W	44-0
Nov. 18	at Buffalo	W	17-0
Nov. 22	at Dallas	W	14-7
Dec. 3	PITTSBURGH	W	30-26
Dec. 9	at Baltimore	L	3-16
Dec. 15	DETROIT	W	34-7

AFC DIVISIONAL PLAYOFF

Dec. 23	CINCINNATI	W	34-16

AFC CHAMPIONSHIP

Dec. 30	OAKLAND	W	27-10

SUPER BOWL VIII (IN HOUSTON)

Jan. 13, 1974	Minnesota	W	24-7

▲ Above, Dolphins running back Mercury Morris (22) eludes Vikings tackle Grady Alderman in Super Bowl VIII.

At right, the Dolphins' defense brings down Vikings running back Chuck Foreman in Miami's 24-7 Super Bowl win. ▶

1974

REGULAR SEASON: WON 11, LOST 3
Finished first in AFC East
HEAD COACH: Don Shula

FB Larry Csonka, RB Jim Kiick and WR Paul Warfield left for the rival World Football League after the season.

The Dolphins' attempt to become the first NFL team to reach four consecutive Super Bowls and win three in a row was derailed in Oakland. With less than a minute left and the Dolphins ahead 26-21, Ken Stabler and the Raiders drove to the Miami 8, where it was first-and-goal. With DE Vern Den Herder wrapping up his feet, a falling Stabler lobbed a pass toward the left side of the end zone, where running back Clarence Davis outfought linebacker Mike Kolen for the ball, and the Raiders somehow grabbed a 28-26 lead with 24 seconds left.

Only two of the Dolphins' regular-season games in 1974 drew fewer fans than the playoff game in Oakland and its 52,817 spectators.

Sept. 15	at New England	L	24-34
Sept. 22	**at Buffalo**	**W**	**24-16**
Sept. 29	**at San Diego**	**W**	**28-21**
Oct. 7	**NEW YORK JETS**	**W**	**21-17**
Oct. 13	at Washington	L	17-20
Oct. 20	**KANSAS CITY**	**W**	**9-3**
Oct. 27	**BALTIMORE**	**W**	**17-7**
Nov. 3	**ATLANTA**	**W**	**42-7**
Nov. 10	**at New Orleans**	**W**	**21-0**
Nov. 17	**BUFFALO**	**W**	**35-28**
Nov. 24	at New York Jets	L	14-17
Dec. 2	**CINCINNATI**	**W**	**24-3**
Dec. 8	**at Baltimore**	**W**	**17-16**
Dec. 15	**NEW ENGLAND**	**W**	**34-27**

AFC DIVISIONAL PLAYOFF

Dec. 21	at Oakland	L	26-28

1975

REGULAR SEASON: WON 10, LOST 4
Finished second in AFC East
HEAD COACH: Don Shula

The Dolphins' 31-game winning streak at the Orange Bowl ended with a 31-21 loss to Oakland.

The new-look Dolphins offense had a good season, scoring 30 more points than the previous year's team, as fullback Don Nottingham more than capably replaced Larry Csonka, averaging 4.3 yards per rush and bowling into the end zone 12 times.

Miami became the first 10-4 team in the AFC to miss the NFL playoffs. It was the first time in six years under Don Shula the Dolphins missed the playoffs.

Sept. 22	OAKLAND	L	21-31
Sept. 28	at New England	W	22-14
Oct. 5	at Green Bay	W	31-7
Oct. 12	PHILADELPHIA	W	24-16
Oct. 19	at New York Jets	W	43-0
Oct. 26	at Buffalo	W	35-30
Nov. 2	at Chicago	W	46-13
Nov. 9	NEW YORK JETS	W	27-7
Nov. 16	at Houston	L	19-20
Nov. 23	BALTIMORE	L	17-33
Dec. 1	NEW ENGLAND	W	20-7
Dec. 7	BUFFALO	W	31-21
Dec. 14	at Baltimore	L	7-10 (OT)
Dec. 20	DENVER	W	14-13

1976

REGULAR SEASON: WON 6, LOST 8
Finished third in AFC East
HEAD COACH: Don Shula

Bob Griese had his first season with more interceptions (12) than touchdowns (11) since 1970.

For the first time in coach Don Shula's tenure, the Dolphins allowed more points (264) than they scored (263). The defense had softened and logged a franchise-low 20 sacks, with the leading sackers being Don Reese and Bill Stanfill with four each. It is the lowest total in a non-strike year for a Miami leading sacker.

The Dolphins also set a franchise low for interceptions in a season with 11, and opposing quarterbacks had a gaudy-for-that-era 89.0 passer rating against Miami's defense.

Sept. 13	at Buffalo	W	30-21
Sept. 19	at New England	L	14-30
Sept. 26	NEW YORK JETS	W	16-0
Oct. 3	LOS ANGELES	L	28-31
Oct. 10	at Baltimore	L	14-28
Oct. 17	KANSAS CITY	L	17-20 (OT)
Oct. 24	at Tampa Bay	W	23-20
Oct. 31	NEW ENGLAND	W	10-3
Nov. 7	at New York Jets	W	27-7
Nov. 14	at Pittsburgh	L	3-14
Nov. 22	BALTIMORE	L	16-17
Nov. 28	at Cleveland	L	13-17
Dec. 5	BUFFALO	W	45-27
Dec. 11	MINNESOTA	L	7-29

◄ Dolphins running back Mercury Morris is upended by Raiders safety Jack Tatum in 1975.

1977

REGULAR SEASON: WON 10, LOST 4
Finished second in AFC East
HEAD COACH: Don Shula

Bob Griese became the first quarterback to wear eyeglasses during a game when a problem with his contact lenses arose. A pair of the eyeglasses he wore while playing is on display at the Pro Football Hall of Fame.

For the second time in three years, Miami was locked out of the playoffs despite a 10-4 record. The Dolphins are the only franchise in the Super Bowl era to twice miss the playoffs despite a winning percentage of over .700.

The Dolphins were off to an excellent start and, with a 5-1 record, were leading the San Diego Chargers 13-7 with seconds left. However, Chargers quarterback James Harris fooled everyone in the Orange Bowl with a naked bootleg for a 5-yard touchdown. Rolf Benirschke's extra point gave the Chargers the win, Miami's lone defeat at home and a dagger when the Dolphins came up short in the tiebreaker with the Baltimore Colts for the AFC East title and the playoffs.

Sept. 18	at Buffalo	W	13-0
Sept. 25	at San Francisco	W	19-15
Oct. 2	HOUSTON	W	27-7
Oct. 9	at Baltimore	L	28-45
Oct. 16	NEW YORK JETS	W	21-17
Oct. 23	SEATTLE	W	31-13
Oct. 30	SAN DIEGO	L	13-14
Nov. 6	at New York Jets	W	14-10
Nov. 13	NEW ENGLAND	W	17-5
Nov. 20	at Cincinnati	L	17-23
Nov. 24	at St. Louis	W	55-14
Dec. 5	BALTIMORE	W	17-6
Dec. 11	at New England	L	10-14
Dec. 17	BUFFALO	W	31-14

◀ Linebacker Steve Towle (56) is emotional after the defense stopped the Oilers on downs in a 27-7 win in 1977.

At top right, Denny Sym, known as "Dolfan Denny," watches a rare home loss in 1978.

1978

REGULAR SEASON: WON 11, LOST 5
Finished second in AFC East
HEAD COACH: Don Shula

The highlight of the season was the defending Super Bowl champion Dallas Cowboys coming to the Orange Bowl and the Dolphins defeating them 23-16 behind two interceptions and four forced fumbles, three of which Miami recovered.

After four nondescript seasons as a clipboard-holder on the Dolphins sideline, quarterback Don Strock truly started building his credentials as one of the NFL's better backup QBs in 1978, starting seven games and winning five in the stead of injured Bob Griese. Strock threw 12 touchdown passes against six interceptions.

Kicker Garo Yepremian tied a then-NFL record with his 16th consecutive field goal in a win against New England.

Sept. 3	at New York Jets	L	20-33
Sept. 10	at Baltimore	W	42-0
Sept. 17	BUFFALO	W	31-24
Sept. 24	at Philadelphia	L	3-17
Oct. 1	ST. LOUIS	W	24-10
Oct. 9	CINCINNATI	W	21-0
Oct. 15	at San Diego	W	28-21
Oct. 22	at New England	L	24-33
Oct. 29	BALTIMORE	W	26-8
Nov. 5	DALLAS	W	23-16
Nov. 12	at Buffalo	W	25-24
Nov. 20	at Houston	L	30-35
Nov. 26	NEW YORK JETS	L	13-24
Dec. 3	at Washington	W	16-0
Dec. 10	OAKLAND	W	23-6
Dec. 18	NEW ENGLAND	W	23-3

AFC WILD-CARD PLAYOFF

Dec. 24	HOUSTON	L	9-17

Dolphins fullback Larry Csonka protects the ball on a gain against the Saints in 1979.

1979

REGULAR SEASON: WON 10, LOST 6
Finished first in AFC East
HEAD COACH: Don Shula

On Oct. 14, the Dolphins beat the Buffalo Bills 17-7 in the Orange Bowl, making Miami 20-0 against Buffalo in the 1970s. The Bills won the 1980 season opener. It stands as the longest streak by one NFL team against another.

Despite no longer being the dominating player he was early in the decade, Larry Csonka returned to the Dolphins after a four-season absence and scored 13 touchdowns, by far his most in Miami (his previous high had been nine in 1974). It was his final NFL season.

The Dolphins played in front of a crowd of more than 80,000 for the first time in franchise history when they visited Cleveland on Nov. 18.

Sept. 2	at Buffalo	W	9-7
Sept. 9	SEATTLE	W	19-10
Sept. 16	at Minnesota	W	27-12
Sept. 23	CHICAGO	W	31-16
Sept. 30	at New York Jets	L	27-33
Oct. 8	at Oakland	L	3-13
Oct. 14	BUFFALO	W	17-7
Oct. 21	at New England	L	13-28
Oct. 28	GREEN BAY	W	27-7
Nov. 5	HOUSTON	L	6-9
Nov. 11	BALTIMORE	W	19-0
Nov. 18	at Cleveland	L	24-30 (OT)
Nov. 25	at Baltimore	W	28-24
Nov. 29	NEW ENGLAND	W	39-24
Dec. 9	at Detroit	W	28-10
Dec. 15	NEW YORK JETS	L	24-27

AFC DIVISIONAL PLAYOFF

| Dec. 30 | at Pittsburgh | L | 14-34 |

1980

REGULAR SEASON: WON 8, LOST 8
Finished third in AFC East
HEAD COACH: Don Shula

In the second game of the season, Don Shula was staring at an 0-2 start for the first time in his career as the Dolphins trailed the Cincinnati Bengals 16-7 after a safety with 6:21 left in the game. Instead of the traditional punt following a safety, Shula had punter George Roberts squib it off his foot, knowing that this was the one time when a punt is a live ball after 10 yards. The Bengals were fooled and the Dolphins recovered. A couple of more non-traditional plays propelled Miami to the 17-16 escape.

After registering his 100th win when he came off the bench and threw two fourth-quarter TDs on Sept. 21, Bob Griese saw the end of his 14-year Dolphins career. After his throwing shoulder was injured against the Colts in the Orange Bowl on Oct. 5, David Woodley and Don Strock became the Miami quarterback tandem for almost three seasons.

For the final game of the season, a Saturday matchup between the 8-7 Dolphins and 3-12 New York Jets, NBC decided to spice up interest in the dreary affair by televising the game without announcers. So, with only the ambient noise from the Orange Bowl being piped in, the Jets upset the Dolphins 24-17.

Sept. 7	at Buffalo	L	7-17
Sept. 14	CINCINNATI	W	17-16
Sept. 21	at Atlanta	W	20-17
Sept. 28	NEW ORLEANS	W	21-16
Oct. 5	BALTIMORE	L	17-30
Oct. 12	at New England	L	0-34
Oct. 19	BUFFALO	W	17-14
Oct. 27	at New York Jets	L	14-17
Nov. 2	at Oakland	L	10-16
Nov. 9	at Los Angeles	W	35-14
Nov. 16	SAN FRANCISCO	W	17-13
Nov. 20	SAN DIEGO	L	24-27 (OT)
Nov. 30	at Pittsburgh	L	10-23
Dec. 8	NEW ENGLAND	W	16-13 (OT)
Dec. 14	at Baltimore	W	24-14
Dec. 20	NEW YORK JETS	L	17-24

1981

REGULAR SEASON: WON 11, LOST 4, TIED 1
Finished first in AFC East
HEAD COACH: Don Shula

WR Duriel Harris was in the midst of his finest Dolphins season when he injured his leg while jumping in a TD celebration against the Philadelphia Eagles. He missed the final three regular-season games and a sure 1,000-yard season, since he had 911 yards when injured.

In the third quarter of a Monday night game with the Eagles leading 10-3, the closed, east end of the Orange Bowl was so loud that Philly QB Ron Jaworski stepped back from the center to wait for a lull in the noise. Each time he approached the center, the din became more deafening. After about a half-dozen tries, he ran the play, and his pass was intercepted by Lyle Blackwood. The Dolphins won 13-10.

In one of the NFL's great postseason games, relief QB Don Strock helped whittle the Chargers' 24-0 lead down to 24-10 with the Dolphins at the San Diego 40 and six seconds left in the first half. After a timeout, Strock threw 20 yards to Harris, who pitched to Tony Nathan, who ran in untouched for the final 25 yards. The Dolphins went into halftime down 24-17 at the Orange Bowl. The Dolphins lost 41-38 in overtime, but the game achieved sports immortality.

Sept. 6	at St. Louis	W	20-7
Sept. 10	PITTSBURGH	W	30-10
Sept. 20	at Houston	W	16-10
Sept. 27	at Baltimore	W	31-28
Oct. 4	NEW YORK JETS	T	28-28 (OT)
Oct. 12	at Buffalo	L	21-31
Oct. 18	WASHINGTON	W	13-10
Oct. 25	at Dallas	L	27-28
Nov. 1	BALTIMORE	W	27-10
Nov. 8	at New England	W	30-27 (OT)
Nov. 15	OAKLAND	L	17-33
Nov. 22	at New York Jets	L	15-16
Nov. 30	PHILADELPHIA	W	13-10
Dec. 6	NEW ENGLAND	W	24-14
Dec. 13	at Kansas City	W	17-7
Dec. 19	BUFFALO	W	16-6

AFC DIVISIONAL PLAYOFF

Jan. 2, 1982	SAN DIEGO	L	38-41 (OT)

1982

REGULAR SEASON: WON 7, LOST 2
Finished second in AFC
HEAD COACH: Don Shula

After the Dolphins' victory over Baltimore on Sept. 19, NFL players embarked on a 57-day strike. After it ended, the league returned to action on Nov. 21 for a nine-game regular season. The Dolphins were 3-0 before the strike and 4-2 afterward.

With 4:45 left in a scoreless, snowbound Dec. 12 game, New England coach Ron Meyer ordered a convict out on work-release, Mark Henderson, to drive a snowplow on the field and clear a spot for the winning field-goal attempt. Officials initially thought Henderson was clearing snow for a first-down measurement. Henderson veered to clear snow from where John Smith kicked the 33-yard field goal. Dolphins coach Don Shula immediately protested the game, to no avail. The John Deere tractor Henderson drove now graces in the Patriots' Hall of Fame.

With the Dolphins up 17-13 late in the third quarter of Super Bowl XVII against Washington, Kim Bokamper batted Redskins QB Joe Theismann's pass into the air. Bokamper could have had an interception and touchdown, but Theismann leaped and smacked the ball, creating an incompletion. Instead of a large lead that could have shut down the Redskins' run game, Miami watched John Riggins carry the ball 13 times the fourth quarter. The Dolphins lost 27-17.

Sept. 12	at New York Jets	W	45-28
Sept. 19	BALTIMORE	W	24-20
Nov. 21	at Buffalo	W	9-7
Nov. 29	at Tampa Bay	L	17-23
Dec. 5	MINNESOTA	W	22-14
Dec. 12	at New England	L	0-3
Dec. 18	NEW YORK JETS	W	20-19
Dec. 27	BUFFALO	W	27-10
Jan. 2, 1983	at Baltimore	W	34-7

AFC WILD-CARD PLAYOFF
Jan. 8	NEW ENGLAND	W	28-13

AFC DIVISIONAL PLAYOFF
Jan. 16	SAN DIEGO	W	34-13

AFC CHAMPIONSHIP
Jan. 23	NEW YORK JETS	W	14-0

SUPER BOWL XVII (IN PASADENA)
Jan. 30	Washington	L	17-27

Miami's Gerald Small watches Washington's Alvin Garrett haul in a second-quarter touchdown in Super Bowl XVII.

1983

REGULAR SEASON: WON 12, LOST 4
Finished first in AFC East
HEAD COACH: Don Shula

Selecting 27th in the draft, the Dolphins somehow had Dan Marino fall to them, as quarterbacks John Elway (first to the Colts then traded to the Broncos), Todd Blackledge (seventh to the Chiefs), Jim Kelly (14th to the Bills), Tony Eason (15th to the Patriots) and Ken O'Brien (24th to the Jets) were selected ahead of the Pitt signal-caller.

Marino piled up 20 touchdown passes against six interceptions in a little more than nine games his rookie year. He debuted on Sept. 19, in the fourth quarter of a Raiders blowout of Miami on a Monday night in Los Angeles. Marino's first start was Oct. 9 in the Orange Bowl against Buffalo. He missed the final two regular-season games after injuring his knee in Houston. He returned for the home playoff game against Seattle, a 27-20 loss in a constant rain.

Marino's plummet in the draft paled compared with future star receiver Mark Clayton's. The Louisville wideout was passed over 222 times before getting the call from Miami.

Sept. 4	at Buffalo	W	12-0
Sept. 11	**NEW ENGLAND**	W	34-24
Sept. 19	at L.A. Raiders	L	14-27
Sept. 25	**KANSAS CITY**	W	14-6
Oct. 2	at New Orleans	L	7-17
Oct. 9	BUFFALO	L	35-38 (OT)
Oct. 16	**at New York Jets**	W	32-14
Oct. 23	**at Baltimore**	W	21-7
Oct. 30	**L.A. RAMS**	W	30-14
Nov. 6	**at San Francisco**	W	20-17
Nov. 13	at New England	L	6-17
Nov. 20	**BALTIMORE**	W	37-0
Nov. 28	**CINCINNATI**	W	38-14
Dec. 4	**at Houston**	W	24-17
Dec. 10	**ATLANTA**	W	31-24
Dec. 16	**NEW YORK JETS**	W	34-14

AFC DIVISIONAL PLAYOFF

Dec. 31	SEATTLE	L	20-27

Dolphins tight end Dan Johnson, at top, is foiled on a pass attempt. Above, Johnson signals a touchdown after QB Dan Marino (13) scored.

1984

REGULAR SEASON: WON 14, LOST 2
Finished first in AFC East
HEAD COACH: Don Shula

Although Dan Marino's 48 touchdown passes of 1984 have been edged out in the record books a couple times since, remember this: In Marino's sophomore year in the NFL, he broke the previous season TD-pass record (Johnny Unitas' 36) by 33 percent.

In the AFC Championship Game against the Pittsburgh Steelers, Marino sliced and diced the Steelers with one perfectly thrown vertical route after another. Marino finished with an average of more than 20 yards per completion as he threw for 421 yards and four touchdowns to earn a Super Bowl XIX matchup with the San Francisco 49ers. Unfortunately, that game was a 38-16 dismantling by Joe Montana and Co., in Miami's last visit to the Super Bowl.

Sept. 2	at Washington	W	35-17
Sept. 9	NEW ENGLAND	W	28-7
Sept. 17	at Buffalo	W	21-17
Sept. 23	INDIANAPOLIS	W	44-7
Sept. 30	at St. Louis	W	36-28
Oct. 7	at Pittsburgh	W	31-7
Oct. 14	HOUSTON	W	28-10
Oct. 21	at New England	W	44-24
Oct. 28	BUFFALO	W	38-7
Nov. 4	at New York Jets	W	31-17
Nov. 11	PHILADELPHIA	W	24-23
Nov. 18	at San Diego	L	28-34 (OT)
Nov. 26	NEW YORK JETS	W	28-17
Dec. 2	L.A. RAIDERS	L	34-45
Dec. 9	at Indianapolis	W	35-17
Dec. 17	DALLAS	W	28-21

AFC DIVISIONAL PLAYOFF

Dec. 29	SEATTLE	W	31-10

AFC CHAMPIONSHIP

Jan. 6, 1985	PITTSBURGH	W	45-28

SUPER BOWL XIX (IN PALO ALTO)

Jan. 20	San Francisco	L	16-38

Quarterback Dan Marino is sacked by the 49ers' Jeff Stover in Marino's only Super Bowl appearance, a 38-16 loss in 1985.

1985

REGULAR SEASON: WON 12, LOST 4
Finished first in AFC East
HEAD COACH: Don Shula

With the legacy of the 1972 perfect team in jeopardy, the Dolphins faced the 12-0 Chicago Bears in December. Chicago had allowed an average of 7.6 points in its previous nine games, but the Dolphins surpassed that with a 10-7 lead after the first quarter. The Dolphins piled up three more TDs before halftime, and the 1972 Dolphins – some on the Orange Bowl sideline wearing their aqua alumni jackets – remained alone in their perfection.

In a rain-soaked AFC Championship Game at home, the Dolphins fumbled five times, losing four of them, and Dan Marino tossed two interceptions as the opportunistic New England Patriots won 31-14. It was Miami's first loss in an AFC title game in six tries.

Sept. 8	at Houston	L	23-26
Sept. 15	INDIANAPOLIS	W	30-13
Sept. 22	KANSAS CITY	W	31-0
Sept. 29	at Denver	W	30-26
Oct. 6	PITTSBURGH	W	24-20
Oct. 14	at New York Jets	L	7-23
Oct. 20	TAMPA BAY	W	41-38
Oct. 27	at Detroit	L	21-31
Nov. 3	at New England	L	13-17
Nov. 10	NEW YORK JETS	W	21-17
Nov. 17	at Indianapolis	W	34-20
Nov. 24	at Buffalo	W	23-14
Dec. 2	CHICAGO	W	38-24
Dec. 8	at Green Bay	W	34-24
Dec. 16	NEW ENGLAND	W	30-27
Dec. 22	BUFFALO	W	28-0

AFC DIVISIONAL PLAYOFF

Jan. 4, 1986	CLEVELAND	W	24-21

AFC CHAMPIONSHIP

Jan. 11	NEW ENGLAND	L	14-31

1986

REGULAR SEASON: WON 8, LOST 8
Finished third in AFC East
HEAD COACH: Don Shula

The defense, for the fourth consecutive year, allowed more points than the year before and the difference between 1985 (320) and 1986 (405) was 5.3 points per game.

In a game in New Jersey against the Jets, Dan Marino threw six touchdown passes and inconceivably lost 51-45 in OT. His counterpart, Ken O'Brien, threw for 479 yards and four TDs. Marino tied Bob Griese's team record for TD passes in one game.

The 21-season run at the Orange Bowl came to an end with a whimper as the New England Patriots won 34-27 to send the Dolphins to a non-winning record for only the second time under Don Shula. The Patriots had lost their first 16 games in the Orange Bowl against the Shula-coached Dolphins, but won their final two.

Sept. 7	at San Diego	L	28-50
Sept. 14	INDIANAPOLIS	W	30-10
Sept. 21	at New York Jets	L	45-51 (OT)
Sept. 28	SAN FRANCISCO	L	16-31
Oct. 5	at New England	L	7-34
Oct. 12	BUFFALO	W	27-14
Oct. 19	L.A. RAIDERS	L	28-30
Oct. 26	at Indianapolis	W	17-13
Nov. 2	HOUSTON	W	28-7
Nov. 10	at Cleveland	L	16-26
Nov. 16	at Buffalo	W	34-24
Nov. 24	NEW YORK JETS	W	45-3
Nov. 30	ATLANTA	L	14-20
Dec. 7	at New Orleans	W	31-27
Dec. 14	at L.A. Rams	W	37-31 (OT)
Dec. 22	NEW ENGLAND	L	27-34

QB Dan Marino endures the celebratory gestures of ▶
Patriots linebacker Don Blackmon in a 1986 defeat.

Coach Don Shula gathers the team before overtime in a 1987 game vs. Buffalo. The Dolphins lost 34-31.

1987

REGULAR SEASON: WON 8, LOST 7
Finished second in AFC East

HEAD COACH: Don Shula

After Week 2 of the season, the players began a strike. Week 3 was canceled, but owners quickly cobbled together teams of replacement players, with whom the league played for the next three weeks. The strike ended in time for full resumption by Week 7. The Dolphins went 1-2 with their replacement players.

An Oct. 11 42-0 rout of the Kansas City Chiefs, played with replacement players, was the first regular-season NFL game played at Joe Robbie Stadium.

The Dolphins were shut out by the Buffalo Bills 27-0 in November, ending Dan Marino's streak of 30 consecutive games with at least one TD pass.

Sept. 13	at New England	L	21-28
Sept. 20	**at Indianapolis**	**W**	**23-10**
*Oct. 4	at Seattle	L	20-24
*Oct. 11	**KANSAS CITY**	**W**	**42-0**
*Oct. 18	at New York Jets	L	31-37 (OT)
Oct. 25	BUFFALO	L	31-34 (OT)
Nov. 1	**PITTSBURGH**	**W**	**35-24**
Nov. 8	**at Cincinnati**	**W**	**20-14**
Nov. 15	INDIANAPOLIS	L	21-40
Nov. 22	**at Dallas**	**W**	**20-14**
Nov. 29	at Buffalo	L	0-27
Dec. 7	**NEW YORK JETS**	**W**	**37-28**
Dec. 13	**at Philadelphia**	**W**	**28-10**
Dec. 20	**WASHINGTON**	**W**	**23-21**
Dec. 28	NEW ENGLAND	L	10-24

* With replacement players during strike

1988

REGULAR SEASON: WON 6, LOST 10
Finished fifth in AFC East

HEAD COACH: Don Shula

Don Shula endured the lone double-digit-loss season in his 33 years on the NFL sideline. Yet, at one point in the season, the Dolphins were 5-4.

The Dolphins played abroad for the first time, defeating the San Francisco 49ers 27-21 in a preseason game in London in front of 70,525 fans.

Dan Marino saw his passer rating go down as he threw balls away and avoided sacks like no one ever has. In 612 dropbacks, Marino was brought down a minuscule six times (once every 102 dropbacks). The only quarterback who has ever been within shouting distance of that number (with at least 550 dropbacks) was the Lions' Joey Harrington in 2003, who was brought down nine times in 563 dropbacks (once every 62.6).

Sept. 4	at Chicago	L	7-34
Sept. 11	at Buffalo	L	6-9
Sept. 18	**GREEN BAY**	**W**	**24-17**
Sept. 25	at Indianapolis	L	13-15
Oct. 2	**MINNESOTA**	**W**	**24-7**
Oct. 9	**at L.A. Raiders**	**W**	**24-14**
Oct. 16	**SAN DIEGO**	**W**	**31-28**
Oct. 23	NEW YORK JETS	L	30-44
Oct. 30	**at Tampa Bay**	**W**	**17-14**
Nov. 6	at New England	L	10-21
Nov. 14	BUFFALO	L	6-31
Nov. 20	NEW ENGLAND	L	3-6
Nov. 27	at New York Jets	L	34-38
Dec. 4	INDIANAPOLIS	L	28-31
Dec. 12	**CLEVELAND**	**W**	**38-31**
Dec. 18	at Pittsburgh	L	24-40

Top, Dolphins wide receiver Mark Clayton ▶ makes a first-quarter touchdown catch against the Jets in 1988.

At right, versatile receiver Jim Jenson makes a catch against the Vikings in a Miami victory.

1989

REGULAR SEASON: WON 8, LOST 8
Finished second (tied) in AFC East
HEAD COACH: Don Shula

Dan Marino finally had a season in which he played as inconsistently as his surrounding cast, tossing an unsightly 16 interceptions in the season's first eight games as Miami went 4-4. On the plus side, Marino became the 13th player in history to pass for at least 200 career touchdowns, reaching 200 faster than any previous NFL quarterback. He also tied Dan Fouts' NFL record of at least 3,000 yards passing in six seasons.

The Dolphins followed the late-season collapse of 1988 with another one in 1989. The Dolphins were 7-4 and primed to end a three-year absence from the playoffs when the Steelers came to town in November. Miami took a 14-0 lead into the second quarter, and then the game unraveled – and perhaps the season, too – with 34 unanswered Pittsburgh points. The culprit: five turnovers, all inside Dolphins territory, combined with a Marino shoulder injury.

Sept. 10	BUFFALO	L	24-27
Sept. 17	at New England	W	24-10
Sept. 24	NEW YORK JETS	L	33-40
Oct. 1	at Houston	L	7-39
Oct. 8	CLEVELAND	W	13-10 (OT)
Oct. 15	at Cincinnati	W	20-13
Oct. 22	GREEN BAY	W	23-20
Oct. 29	at Buffalo	L	17-31
Nov. 5	INDIANAPOLIS	W	19-13
Nov. 12	at New York Jets	W	31-23
Nov. 19	at Dallas	W	17-14
Nov. 26	PITTSBURGH	L	14-34
Dec. 3	at Kansas City	L	21-26
Dec. 10	NEW ENGLAND	W	31-10
Dec. 17	at Indianapolis	L	13-42
Dec. 24	KANSAS CITY	L	24-27

◀ The Chiefs' defense sacks Dolphins QB Dan Marino in the second quarter of Miami's 26-21 loss in 1989.

1990

REGULAR SEASON: WON 12, LOST 4
Finished second in AFC East
HEAD COACH: Don Shula

Team owner and founder Joe Robbie died at 73. Later, Blockbuster executive H. Wayne Huizenga bought half ownership in the Joe Robbie Stadium Corp. and 15 percent ownership in the team.

The defense became the Dolphins' strength for the first time in the Dan Marino era, allowing 242 points (15.1 per game).

In the first Dolphins playoff game at Joe Robbie Stadium, they were down 16-3 to the Kansas City Chiefs with less than 13 minutes left. After a 1-yard TD pass from Marino to Tony Paige, the Dolphins completed the comeback as Marino fired to Mark Clayton in the right flat. Chiefs CB Albert Lewis went for the interception, but Marino's arm was too strong, and Clayton scored with 3:28 left in what was a one-point victory.

Sept. 9	at New England	W	27-24
Sept. 16	BUFFALO	W	30-7
Sept. 23	at New York Giants	L	3-20
Sept. 30	at Pittsburgh	W	28-6
Oct. 7	NEW YORK JETS	W	20-16
Oct. 18	NEW ENGLAND	W	17-10
Oct. 28	at Indianapolis	W	27-7
Nov. 4	PHOENIX	W	23-3
Nov. 11	at New York Jets	W	17-3
Nov. 19	L.A. RAIDERS	L	10-13
Nov. 25	at Cleveland	W	30-13
Dec. 2	at Washington	L	20-42
Dec. 9	PHILADELPHIA	W	23-20 (OT)
Dec. 16	SEATTLE	W	24-17
Dec. 23	at Buffalo	L	14-24
Dec. 30	INDIANAPOLIS	W	23-17

AFC WILD-CARD PLAYOFF

Jan. 5, 1991	KANSAS CITY	W	17-16

AFC DIVISIONAL PLAYOFF

Jan. 12	at Buffalo	L	34-44

Dolphins wide receiver Mark Duper reaches for the end zone in Miami's 23-20 overtime loss to the Jets in 1991.

1991

REGULAR SEASON: WON 8, LOST 8
Finished second in AFC East
HEAD COACH: Don Shula

On a Monday night game against the visiting Cincinnati Bengals, the world met Bryan Cox. After the Dolphins kicked off in the third quarter, ahead 20-6, Cincinnati linebacker Alex Gordon laid out kicker Pete Stoyanovich. Cox, a rookie linebacker from East St. Louis, stormed the Cincinnati side-line, challenging the whole team seemingly to fight. Miami went on to a 37-13 win.

In a December game against the Tampa Bay Bucs, Dan Marino surpassed 3,000 passing yards for the season for the eighth time in his career, setting an NFL record.

The 8-7 Dolphins and 7-8 Jets met in the regular-season finale in a de facto playoff game: The winner earned the final spot in the AFC playoffs. The Dolphins' run defense allowed 231 yards on 39 carries, but still Miami grabbed the lead late with 44 seconds left in regulation. However, Ken O'Brien hit a couple key passes and set up Raul Allegre to make a tying 44-yard field goal as time expired. Then, in overtime, Johnny Hector, who had 132 rushing yards, carved up Miami, and Allegre, signed only five days earlier by the Jets, eliminated the Dolphins with a 30-yarder.

Sept. 1	at Buffalo	L	31-35
Sept. 8	**INDIANAPOLIS**	**W**	**17-6**
Sept. 15	at Detroit	L	13-17
Sept. 22	**GREEN BAY**	**W**	**16-13**
Sept. 29	at New York Jets	L	23-41
Oct. 6	**at New England**	**W**	**20-10**
Oct. 13	at Kansas City	L	7-42
Oct. 20	HOUSTON	L	13-17
Nov. 3	**at Indianapolis**	**W**	**10-6**
Nov. 10	**NEW ENGLAND**	**W**	**30-20**
Nov. 18	BUFFALO	L	27-41
Nov. 24	**at Chicago**	**W**	**16-13 (OT)**
Dec. 1	**TAMPA BAY**	**W**	**33-14**
Dec. 9	**CINCINNATI**	**W**	**37-13**
Dec. 15	at San Diego	L	30-38
Dec. 22	NEW YORK JETS	L	20-23 (OT)

1992

REGULAR SEASON: WON 11, LOST 5
Finished first in AFC East
HEAD COACH: Don Shula

Jets defensive coordinator Pete Carroll wrapped his hands around his neck in a choking motion after the Dolphins' Pete Stoyanovich missed an extra point with Miami trailing 17-16 late in a December game. However, after a Jets three-and-out, the Dolphins quickly pushed the ball downfield and set up Stoyanovich for another kick. He made this one, and the Jets lost.

The Dolphins' September season-opener at home against the Patriots was postponed in the aftermath of Hurricane Andrew, which walloped South Florida in late August. The game was moved to Oct. 18, and the Dolphins won 38-17.

In their final year with the Dolphins, WRs Mark Clayton and Mark Duper combined for 87 catches, 1,381 yards and 10 TDs. The Marks Brothers finished with a combined 1,061 receptions, 17,512 yards and 140 touchdowns.

Sept. 14	at Cleveland	W	27-23
Sept. 20	L.A. RAMS	W	26-10
Sept. 27	at Seattle	W	19-17
Oct. 4	at Buffalo	W	37-10
Oct. 11	ATLANTA	W	21-17
Oct. 18	NEW ENGLAND	W	38-17
Oct. 25	INDIANAPOLIS	L	20-31
Nov. 1	at New York Jets	L	14-26
Nov. 8	at Indianapolis	W	28-0
Nov. 16	BUFFALO	L	20-26
Nov. 22	HOUSTON	W	19-16
Nov. 29	at New Orleans	L	13-24
Dec. 6	at San Francisco	L	3-27
Dec. 14	L.A. RAIDERS	W	20-7
Dec. 20	NEW YORK JETS	W	19-17
Dec. 27	at New England	W	16-13 (OT)

AFC DIVISIONAL PLAYOFF

Jan. 10, 1993	SAN DIEGO	W	31-0

AFC CHAMPIONSHIP

Jan. 17	BUFFALO	L	10-29

1993

REGULAR SEASON: WON 9, LOST 7
Finished second in AFC East
HEAD COACH: Don Shula

The Dolphins were off to a solid 3-1 start for the season, but while playing the Browns in Cleveland, Dan Marino crumpled to the ground, untouched. A ruptured Achilles' tendon ended his season. Scott Mitchell stepped in, and after his first pass was intercepted and returned for a touchdown, he gained his bearings and led the Dolphins to victory with two second-half TD passes.

Mitchell played sharply in getting Miami to 6-2. However, Mitchell then separated his shoulder while playing the Eagles in Philadelphia. The Dolphins, with Doug Pederson taking snaps, still managed to win at Veterans Stadium 19-14, giving Don Shula his NFL-record 325th career win.

Against Dallas on Thanksgiving, a snow/sleet storm had covered the field with a white sheet. The game came down to Pete Stoyanovich trying a 41-yard field goal. The kick was batted by Jimmy Jones. It trickled past the line of scrimmage and spun on the ground. Once it crossed the line of scrimmage, the Dolphins could not recover the ball unless it was first touched by a Cowboy. Incredibly, Cowboys DT Leon Lett slid after it and kicked the ball. The Dolphins recovered the ball and got one more chance at the kick, which Stoyanovich converted, shocking the powerhouse Cowboys with a win.

Sept. 5	at Indianapolis	W	24-20
Sept. 12	NEW YORK JETS	L	14-24
Sept. 26	at Buffalo	W	22-13
Oct. 4	WASHINGTON	W	17-10
Oct. 10	at Cleveland	W	24-14
Oct. 24	INDIANAPOLIS	W	41-27
Oct. 31	KANSAS CITY	W	30-10
Nov. 7	at New York Jets	L	10-27
Nov. 14	at Philadelphia	W	19-14
Nov. 21	NEW ENGLAND	W	17-13
Nov. 25	at Dallas	W	16-14
Dec. 5	NEW YORK GIANTS	L	14-19
Dec. 13	PITTSBURGH	L	20-21
Dec. 19	BUFFALO	L	34-47
Dec. 27	at San Diego	L	20-45
Jan. 2, 1994	at New England	L	27-33 (OT)

Don Shula celebrates his 325th victory as an NFL coach, Nov. 14, 1993, setting the record for the most wins.

Dan Marino gets a pass off before being hit by a Patriots defender in the opening game of the 1994 season.

1994

REGULAR SEASON: WON 10, LOST 6
Finished first in AFC East
HEAD COACH: Don Shula

In the offseason, H. Wayne Huizenga purchased the remaining interest in the team and the stadium from the Robbie family.

Dan Marino returned from his Achilles' tendon tear after missing 11 games and made up for lost time in the season opener against the New England Patriots. He threw for 473 yards and five touchdowns, including a 35-yard game-winner on fourth down to Irving Fryar for a 39-35 victory.

For the second consecutive year, the Dolphins lost a major offensive cog as running back Terry Kirby blew out his knee in Minnesota. Kirby had racked up 1,264 total yards and six touchdowns as a rookie in 1993. Against the Vikings, the Dolphins attempted a two-point conversion and gave Kirby the ball to run up the middle. He was stacked up and bent over backward, causing the season-ending injury.

Sept. 4	NEW ENGLAND	W	39-35
Sept. 11	Green Bay (at Mil.)	W	24-14
Sept. 18	NEW YORK JETS	W	28-14
Sept. 25	at Minnesota	L	35-38
Oct. 2	at Cincinnati	W	23-7
Oct. 9	at Buffalo	L	11-21
Oct. 16	L.A. RAIDERS	W	20-17 (OT)
Oct. 30	at New England	W	23-3
Nov. 6	INDIANAPOLIS	W	22-21
Nov. 13	CHICAGO	L	14-17
Nov. 20	at Pittsburgh	L	13-16 (OT)
Nov. 27	at New York Jets	W	28-24
Dec. 4	BUFFALO	L	31-42
Dec. 12	KANSAS CITY	W	45-28
Dec. 18	at Indianapolis	L	6-10
Dec. 25	DETROIT	W	27-20

AFC WILD-CARD PLAYOFF

Dec. 31	KANSAS CITY	W	27-17

AFC DIVISIONAL PLAYOFF

Jan. 8, 1995	at San Diego	L	21-22

1995

REGULAR SEASON: WON 9, LOST 7
Finished second (tied) in AFC East
HEAD COACH: Don Shula

As usual, the Dolphins got off to an excellent start in September and took a 4-0 record into a matchup against the Colts at Joe Robbie Stadium. Miami led 24-3 in the second half, but Jim Harbaugh led Indianapolis' comeback with three unanswered touchdowns and then won in overtime. That loss, perhaps as much as any other, created momentum for the end of coach Don Shula's great Miami run. The Dolphins lost their next two games and never found that first-month mojo again.

QB Dan Marino continued setting records, becoming the NFL's all-time career leader in completions when he surpassed 3,686; passing yards when he surpassed 47,003 and career touchdown passes when he bettered the previous record of 342. Shula recorded his final win — for an NFL-record 347 victories — on Dec. 24 against the St. Louis Rams.

Shula's coaching career sadly ended in the chill of Buffalo as the Bills ran through Miami's defense for 341 rushing yards and a 37-22 wild-card win on Dec. 30.

Sept. 3	NEW YORK JETS	W	52-14
Sept. 10	at New England	W	20-3
Sept. 18	PITTSBURGH	W	23-10
Oct. 1	at Cincinnati	W	26-23
Oct. 8	INDIANAPOLIS	L	24-27 (OT)
Oct. 15	at New Orleans	L	30-33
Oct. 22	at N.Y. Jets	L	16-17
Oct. 29	BUFFALO	W	23-6
Nov. 5	at San Diego	W	24-14
Nov. 12	NEW ENGLAND	L	17-34
Nov. 20	SAN FRANCISCO	L	20-44
Nov. 26	at Indianapolis	L	28-36
Dec. 3	ATLANTA	W	21-20
Dec. 11	KANSAS CITY	W	13-6
Dec. 17	at Buffalo	L	20-23
Dec. 24	at St. Louis	W	41-22

AFC WILD-CARD PLAYOFF

Dec. 30	at Buffalo	L	22-37

Dan Marino hugs former teammate Mark Clayton after breaking the NFL record with his 343rd career touchdown pass on Nov. 26, 1995.

1996

REGULAR SEASON: WON 8, LOST 8
Finished fourth in AFC East
HEAD COACH: Jimmy Johnson

On Jan. 5, Don Shula resigned from the Miami Dolphins at age 66, finishing his unparalleled NFL career with 347 wins in 33 seasons. The only coach within shouting distance of that total is the New England Patriots' Bill Belichick, who won 233 games in his first 20 seasons. If he won 12 games per year going forward, Belichick would need to coach 10 more seasons, or until he is 72.

In a move that had been loudly desired by a faction of Dolphins fans for a year, Jimmy Johnson took the reins of the Dolphins. The coach who won a national title with the Miami Hurricanes and two Super Bowls with the Dallas Cowboys began overhauling the roster, especially the defense, and installing a more balanced offensive philosophy (in 1995, the Dolphins dropped back to pass 621 times and ran 413 times; In 1996 Johnson narrowed that gap to 540 dropbacks and 460 runs).

With the 154th pick in his first Dolphins draft, Johnson selected a diminutive but quick and smart linebacker out of Texas Tech named Zach Thomas. So impressive was Thomas in training camp that Johnson cut one of his old favorites, Jack Del Rio, after the exhibition opener.

Sept. 1	NEW ENGLAND	W	24-10
Sept. 8	at Arizona	W	38-10
Sept. 15	NEW YORK JETS	W	36-27
Sept. 23	at Indianapolis	L	6-10
Oct. 6	SEATTLE	L	15-22
Oct. 13	at Buffalo	W	21-7
Oct. 20	at Philadelphia	L	28-35
Oct. 27	DALLAS	L	10-29
Nov. 3	at New England	L	23-42
Nov. 10	INDIANAPOLIS	W	37-13
Nov. 17	at Houston	W	23-20
Nov. 25	PITTSBURGH	L	17-24
Dec. 1	at Oakland	L	7-17
Dec. 8	NEW YORK GIANTS	L	7-17
Dec. 16	BUFFALO	W	16-14
Dec. 22	at New York Jets	W	31-28

Newly retired Don Shula is honored for his coaching record while riding with his wife in the 1996 Orange Bowl Parade.

1997

REGULAR SEASON: WON 9, LOST 7
Finished second in AFC East
HEAD COACH: Jimmy Johnson

The Dolphins had five prime-time games in coach Jimmy Johnson's second season, but one of them was not scheduled initially. When the Florida Marlins went to seven games in the World Series against the Cleveland Indians, the Dolphins' game against the Chicago Bears was pushed back a day. The Dolphins had a 33-18 lead with less than 6 minutes left, but Bears QB Erik Kramer led two touchdown drives and, with 1:25 left, converted the tying two-point conversion. The Bears won 36-33 in overtime.

Patriots linebacker Todd Collins ran back a Dan Marino interception for a touchdown in New England's 17-3 playoff win over the Dolphins, and that became one of the most infamous images in Dolphins history. It was obvious that the Patriots knew the Dolphins audibles and rolled their defense into the passing lanes on the game's most pivotal play. Long-time Dolphins offensive coordinator Gary Stevens was fired after the game and uttered his memorable parting line about how he couldn't "make chicken salad out of chicken s---."

Aug. 31	INDIANAPOLIS	W	16-10
Sept. 7	TENNESSEE	W	16-13 (OT)
Sept. 14	at Green Bay	L	18-23
Sept. 21	at Tampa Bay	L	21-31
Oct. 5	KANSAS CITY	W	17-14
Oct. 12	at New York Jets	W	31-20
Oct. 19	at Baltimore	W	24-13
Oct. 27	CHICAGO	L	33-36 (OT)
Nov. 2	at Buffalo	L	6-9
Nov. 9	NEW YORK JETS	W	24-17
Nov. 17	BUFFALO	W	30-13
Nov. 23	at New England	L	24-27
Nov. 30	at Oakland	W	34-16
Dec. 7	DETROIT	W	33-30
Dec. 14	at Indianapolis	L	0-41
Dec. 22	NEW ENGLAND	L	12-14

AFC WILD-CARD PLAYOFF

Dec. 28	at New England	L	3-17

Jimmy Johnson runs
Dolphins minicamp
before the 1998
season began.

1998

REGULAR SEASON: WON 10, LOST 6
Finished second in AFC East
HEAD COACH: Jimmy Johnson

After the draft, coach Jimmy Johnson infamously compared his third-round draft pick, Larry Shannon, to Randy Moss, the uber-talented receiver he had a chance to pick with the 19th selection. Johnson traded down from 19 and picked running back John Avery at No. 29 instead. Avery ended up a non-factor, and Moss will be a Hall of Famer.

On the positive side, Johnson was good at drafting after the first round. By 1998, he had fully overhauled the Dolphins defense behind a core of four future Pro Bowl selections: LB Zach Thomas (5th round in 1996), DE Jason Taylor (3rd round in 1997), CB Sam Madison (2nd round in 1997) and Patrick Surtain (2nd round in 1998).

O.J. McDuffie finished the season with 90 catches, the first Dolphin to lead the NFL in receptions.

Sept. 6	at Indianapolis	W	24-15
Sept. 13	BUFFALO	W	13-7
Sept. 20	PITTSBURGH	W	21-0
Oct. 4	at N.Y. Jets	L	9-20
Oct. 12	at Jacksonville	L	21-28
Oct. 18	ST. LOUIS	W	14-0
Oct. 25	NEW ENGLAND	W	12-9 (OT)
Nov. 1	at Buffalo	L	24-30
Nov. 8	INDIANAPOLIS	W	27-14
Nov. 15	at Carolina	W	13-9
Nov. 23	at New England	L	23-26
Nov. 29	NEW ORLEANS	W	30-10
Dec. 6	at Oakland	W	27-17
Dec. 13	N.Y. JETS	L	16-21
Dec. 21	DENVER	W	31-21
Dec. 27	at Atlanta	L	16-38

AFC WILD-CARD PLAYOFF

Jan. 2, 1999	BUFFALO	W	24-17

AFC DIVISIONAL PLAYOFF

Jan. 9	at Denver	L	3-38

1999

REGULAR SEASON: WON 9, LOST 7
Finished second in AFC East
HEAD COACH: Jimmy Johnson

Jimmy Johnson experienced a Dolphins second-half-of-the-season collapse for himself when his 8-2 team choked their way to a 1-5 finish, though they still made the postseason. The first game of the slide was a Thanksgiving game in Dallas, where Dan Marino had the worst game of his career, throwing five interceptions and no touchdowns. However, two other losses in the meltdown happened in games where the Dolphins scored more than 30 points.

Marino and company put together a performance in Seattle good enough to break a 27-year postseason road losing streak, winning 20-17 in the final game played in the Kingdome. The defense held Seattle to 32 yards in the second half, and Trace Armstrong had three of Miami's six sacks.

Sept. 13	at Denver	W	38-21
Sept. 19	ARIZONA	W	19-16
Oct. 4	BUFFALO	L	18-23
Oct. 10	at Indianapolis	W	34-31
Oct. 17	at New England	W	31-30
Oct. 24	PHILADELPHIA	W	16-13
Oct. 31	at Oakland	W	16-9
Nov. 7	TENNESSEE	W	17-0
Nov. 14	at Buffalo	L	3-23
Nov. 21	NEW ENGLAND	W	27-17
Nov. 25	at Dallas	L	0-20
Dec. 5	INDIANAPOLIS	L	34-37
Dec. 12	at New York Jets	L	20-28
Dec. 19	SAN DIEGO	W	12-9
Dec. 27	NEW YORK JETS	L	31-38
Jan. 2, 2000	at Washington	L	10-21

AFC WILD-CARD PLAYOFF

Jan. 9	at Seattle	W	20-17

AFC DIVISIONAL PLAYOFF

Jan. 15	at Jacksonville	L	7-62

1999

The final game of Dan Marino's record-setting career was a 62-7 rout of the Dolphins by the Jacksonville Jaguars in the Jan. 15, 2000, divisional round of the playoffs. It was also Jimmy Johnson's last game as an NFL coach.

2000

REGULAR SEASON: WON 11, LOST 5
Finished first in AFC East

HEAD COACH: Dave Wannstedt

Dave Wannstedt was hired as coach, and Jay Fiedler had the unenviable task of following Dan Marino at QB. They did well, save for a historic collapse in New Jersey. The Dolphins blew a 30-7 fourth-quarter lead to the Jets and lost in overtime on Monday night – and then two consecutive losses at home in December.

The Dolphins allowed a mere 226 points, Miami's fewest allowed in a 16-game season.

Lamar Smith, a reclamation project from Seattle, provided one of the great Dolphins postseason performances as he carried the ball a whopping 40 times for 209 yards, including a pinball-like game-ending 17-yarder in overtime. The 23-17 victory over the Indianapolis Colts stands as the most recent Dolphins postseason win.

Sept. 3	SEATTLE	W	23-0
Sept. 10	at Minnesota	L	7-13
Sept. 17	BALTIMORE	W	19-6
Sept. 24	NEW ENGLAND	W	10-3
Oct. 1	at Cincinnati	W	31-16
Oct. 8	BUFFALO	W	22-13
Oct. 23	at New York Jets	L	37-40 (OT)
Oct. 29	GREEN BAY	W	28-20
Nov. 5	at Detroit	W	23-8
Nov. 12	at San Diego	W	17-7
Nov. 19	NEW YORK JETS	L	3-20
Nov. 26	at Indianapolis	W	17-14
Dec. 3	at Buffalo	W	33-6
Dec. 10	TAMPA BAY	L	13-16
Dec. 17	INDIANAPOLIS	L	13-20
Dec. 24	at New England	W	27-24

AFC WILD-CARD PLAYOFF

Dec. 30	INDIANAPOLIS	W	23-17 (OT)

AFC DIVISIONAL PLAYOFF

Jan. 6, 2001	at Oakland	L	0-27

2001

REGULAR SEASON: WON 11, LOST 5
Finished second in AFC East
HEAD COACH: Dave Wannstedt

Wide receiver Chris Chambers made a big rookie splash with 883 receiving yards (18.4-yard average) and seven touchdowns. Those stats could have been much better, as there were a number of times he was well behind the last defender but was overthrown.

Safety Brock Marion set a club record with 45.4 yards per interception return on his five pickoffs, the best return-yardage number among any Dolphin with more than one interception in a season.

Sept. 9	at Tennessee	W	31-23
Sept. 23	OAKLAND	W	18-15
Sept. 30	at St. Louis	L	10-42
Oct. 7	NEW ENGLAND	W	30-10
Oct. 14	at New York Jets	L	17-21
Oct. 28	at Seattle	W	24-20
Nov. 4	CAROLINA	W	23-6
Nov. 11	at Indianapolis	W	27-24
Nov. 18	NEW YORK JETS	L	0-24
Nov. 25	at Buffalo	W	34-27
Dec. 2	DENVER	W	21-10
Dec. 10	INDIANAPOLIS	W	41-6
Dec. 16	at San Francisco	L	0-21
Dec. 22	at New England	L	13-20
Dec. 30	ATLANTA	W	21-14
Jan. 6, 2002	BUFFALO	W	34-7

AFC WILD-CARD PLAYOFF

Jan. 13	BALTIMORE	L	3-20

Top, receiver Chris Chambers cradles a catch against the Panthers' Jimmy Hitchcock in 2001. Bottom, Dolphins defensive back Brock Marion celebrates an interception return for a TD against the Falcons. ▶

◀ Top, quarterback Jay Fiedler tries to escape the grasp of Seattle defender Chad Brown. Bottom, running back Lamar Smith hurdles over Buffalo defenders during a 2000 win.

▲ Dolphins tailback Ricky Williams knocks heads with the Lions' Todd Lyght on his way to a 100-yard game in 2002.

2002

REGULAR SEASON: WON 9, LOST 7
Finished third in AFC East

HEAD COACH: Dave Wannstedt

Running back Ricky Williams, acquired for two first-round draft picks, broke the franchise season rushing record on Dec. 1. He finished the season with 1,853 yards – a mind-blowing 595 yards better than Delvin Williams' 1978 mark. Williams was the first Dolphin to lead the NFL in rushing.

Williams wasn't the only one having a good season. DE Jason Taylor tied the club record with 18.5 sacks. Seven Dolphins were named to the Pro Bowl, the largest number since 1984. However, a 2-6 road record sunk Miami, with losses in the final five contests away from Pro Player Stadium, most painfully the closing games at Minnesota and New England.

QB Jay Fiedler led the Dolphins to a 4-1 start, and then led a last-second winning drive to beat perennial contender Denver in its mile-high thin air on a Sunday night. However, on his final pass of the drive, Fiedler hit his passing hand on a helmet and sustained a chip fracture in his thumb. He missed the next six starts, and the Dolphins had skidded to 7-5 by then.

Date	Opponent	Result	Score
Sept. 8	DETROIT	W	49-21
Sept. 15	at Indianapolis	W	21-13
Sept. 22	NEW YORK JETS	W	30-3
Sept. 29	at Kansas City	L	30-48
Oct. 6	NEW ENGLAND	W	26-13
Oct. 13	at Denver	W	24-22
Oct. 20	BUFFALO	L	10-23
Nov. 4	at Green Bay	L	10-24
Nov. 10	at New York Jets	L	10-13
Nov. 17	BALTIMORE	W	26-7
Nov. 24	SAN DIEGO	W	30-3
Dec. 1	at Buffalo	L	21-38
Dec. 9	CHICAGO	W	27-9
Dec. 15	OAKLAND	W	23-17
Dec. 21	at Minnesota	L	17-20
Dec. 29	at New England	L	24-27 (OT)

2003

REGULAR SEASON: WON 10, LOST 6
Finished second in AFC East
HEAD COACH: Dave Wannstedt

Although the Dolphins won more games in the 2003 season than in 2002, production was starting to drop off in some areas. RB Ricky Williams' yards per carry dropped by 27 percent, from 4.8 yards to 3.5. This season Williams had 442 touches, even more than 2002's 430 touches, and that helped him rack up 1,372 rushing yards. Quarterback Jay Fiedler's passer rating dropped from a personal-best 85.2 in the previous season to a poor 72.4.

One area where the Dolphins did not drop off was in their pass rush, where Jason Taylor and Adewale Ogunleye combined for 28 sacks for the second year in a row. Taylor became the Dolphins' career sack leader, surpassing Bill Stanfill's record of 67.5, which had stood since 1976.

Date	Opponent	Result	Score
Sept. 7	HOUSTON	L	20-21
Sept. 14	at New York Jets	W	21-10
Sept. 21	BUFFALO	W	17-7
Oct. 5	at New York Giants	W	23-10
Oct. 12	at Jacksonville	W	24-10
Oct. 19	NEW ENGLAND	L	13-19 (OT)
Oct. 27	San Diego*	W	26-10
Nov. 2	INDIANAPOLIS	L	17-23
Nov. 9	at Tennessee	L	7-31
Nov. 16	BALTIMORE	W	9-6 (OT)
Nov. 23	WASHINGTON	W	24-23
Nov. 27	at Dallas	W	40-21
Dec. 7	at New England	L	0-12
Dec. 15	PHILADELPHIA	L	27-34
Dec. 21	at Buffalo	W	20-3
Dec. 28	NEW YORK JETS	W	23-21

* In Tempe, Ariz.

Defensive end Jason Taylor does a sack dance in a season-ending win over the Jets.

2004

REGULAR SEASON: WON 4, LOST 12
Finished fourth in AFC East
HEAD COACH, weeks 1-9: Dave Wannstedt
HEAD COACH, weeks 10-16: Jim Bates

RB Ricky Williams went into drug-test-induced "retirement" on July 25, after a positive test for marijuana would have suspended him for four games. Later, Williams said that the Dolphins not upgrading the quarterback position (Jay Fiedler, A.J. Feeley and Sage Rosenfels) also played a major factor in his quitting.

On Oct. 10, kicker Olindo Mare injured himself in warmups before a game at New England, pressing wide receiver Wes Welker into service. Welker made a 29-yard field goal and an extra point, as well as kicking off and returning kicks and punts. He became the first player in NFL history to perform all five duties in a game.

For the first time in franchise history, a coach was let go during the season as Dave Wannstedt departed after a 1-8 start. Defensive coordinator Jim Bates took over for the rest of the season and went 3-4.

Date	Opponent	Result	Score
Sept. 11	TENNESSEE	L	7-17
Sept. 19	at Cincinnati	L	13-16
Sept. 26	PITTSBURGH	L	3-13
Oct. 3	NEW YORK JETS	L	9-17
Oct. 10	at New England	L	10-24
Oct. 17	at Buffalo	L	13-20
Oct. 24	**ST. LOUIS**	**W**	**31-14**
Nov. 1	at New York Jets	L	14-41
Nov. 7	ARIZONA	L	23-24
Nov. 21	at Seattle	L	17-24
Nov. 28	**at San Francisco**	**W**	**24-17**
Dec. 5	BUFFALO	L	32-42
Dec. 12	at Denver	L	17-20
Dec. 20	**NEW ENGLAND**	**W**	**29-28**
Dec. 26	**CLEVELAND**	**W**	**10-7**
Jan. 2, 2005	at Baltimore	L	23-30

◄ Dolphins fans, top, wanted tailback Ricky Williams back during the Sept. 11 game against the Titans. Bottom, Miami coach Dave Wannstedt looks frustrated in the Dolphins' Oct. 10 loss to the Patriots.

Defensive end Jason Taylor gets a sack of Raiders quarterback Kerry Collins in the third quarter.

2005

REGULAR SEASON: WON 9, LOST 7
Finished second in AFC East

HEAD COACH: Nick Saban

Coach Nick Saban, who had won a national championship at Louisiana State University, was signed to a five-year contract. His staff had two future NFL coaches on it: Jason Garrett (Cowboys) and Dan Quinn (Falcons).

RB Ricky Williams requested reinstatement from the NFL and returned to the Dolphins, although he didn't return to his previous staggering stats. He finished the season with 743 yards rushing on 168 carries.

The 49 sacks logged by the Dolphins' defense tied a club record established in 1983.

The Dolphins won their final six games, their longest win streak to end a regular season since a seven-win run concluded the 1985 season.

Date	Opponent	Result	Score
Sept. 11	DENVER	W	34-10
Sept. 18	at New York Jets	L	7-17
Sept. 25	CAROLINA	W	27-24
Oct. 9	at Buffalo	L	14-20
Oct. 16	at Tampa Bay	L	13-27
Oct. 21	KANSAS CITY	L	20-30
Oct. 30	at New Orleans	W	21-6
Nov. 6	ATLANTA	L	10-17
Nov. 13	NEW ENGLAND	L	16-23
Nov. 20	at Cleveland	L	0-22
Nov. 27	at Oakland	W	33-21
Dec. 4	BUFFALO	W	24-23
Dec. 11	at San Diego	W	23-21
Dec. 18	NEW YORK JETS	W	24-20
Dec. 24	TENNESSEE	W	24-10
Jan. 1, 2006	at New England	W	28-26

▲ A frustrated Dolphins fan covers up as Miami loses to Green Bay on Oct. 22, 2006. The team finished 6-10.

2006

REGULAR SEASON: WON 6, LOST 10
Finished fourth in AFC East
HEAD COACH: Nick Saban

The NFL suspends off-and-on-again running back Ricky Williams for at least one year for violating the league's substance-abuse policy.

The one bright spot in the disappointing season was defensive end Jason Taylor, who was named the NFL's Defensive Player of the Year. He piled up 13.5 sacks, had two interceptions — both returned for touchdowns — and had an astounding nine forced fumbles.

By the end of the season, coach Nick Saban had lost more games in two NFL seasons than he had in five years during his national-championship tenure at LSU — and the same number of games he has lost at Alabama over his eight-year run in Tuscaloosa. After denying extensively that he was interested in the coaching vacancy in Alabama, he resigned to take that job.

Sept. 7	at Pittsburgh	L	17-28
Sept. 17	BUFFALO	L	6-16
Sept. 24	**TENNESSEE**	**W**	**13-10**
Oct. 1	at Houston	L	15-17
Oct. 8	at New England	L	10-20
Oct. 15	at New York Jets	L	17-20
Oct. 22	GREEN BAY	L	24-34
Nov. 5	**at Chicago**	**W**	**31-13**
Nov. 12	**KANSAS CITY**	**W**	**13-10**
Nov. 19	**MINNESOTA**	**W**	**24-20**
Nov. 23	**at Detroit**	**W**	**27-10**
Dec. 3	JACKSONVILLE	L	10-24
Dec. 10	**NEW ENGLAND**	**W**	**21-0**
Dec. 17	at Buffalo	L	0-21
Dec. 25	NEW YORK JETS	L	10-13
Dec. 31	at Indianapolis	L	22-27

2007

REGULAR SEASON: WON 1, LOST 15
Finished fourth in AFC East
HEAD COACH: Cam Cameron

San Diego Chargers offensive coordinator Cam Cameron was hired as the Dolphins' new coach.

After serving an 18-month suspension, RB Ricky Williams was reinstated by the NFL in November. He suffered a season-ending injury in the second quarter of his first game back at Pittsburgh.

Thank you, Brian Billick. With 12 seconds left in a December game and down 16-13, the Ravens threw a 9-yard pass to reach the Miami 1. Billick, whose team had gained just 163 rushing yards, decided to kick the tying field goal instead of trying to run for the final yard. Thank you, Matt Stover. The Baltimore kicker missed a 44-yard field-goal attempt in overtime. Three plays later, Cleo Lemon hit Greg Camarillo in stride, scoring a 64-yard touchdown and keeping Miami from going winless for the season.

Sept. 9	at Washington	L	13-16 (OT)
Sept. 16	DALLAS	L	20-37
Sept. 23	at New York Jets	L	28-31
Sept. 30	OAKLAND	L	17-35
Oct. 7	at Houston	L	19-22
Oct. 14	at Cleveland	L	31-41
Oct. 21	NEW ENGLAND	L	28-49
Oct. 28	N.Y. GIANTS (in London)	L	10-13
Nov. 11	BUFFALO	L	10-13
Nov. 18	at Philadelphia	L	7-17
Nov. 26	at Pittsburgh	L	0-3
Dec. 2	NEW YORK JETS	L	13-40
Dec. 9	at Buffalo	L	17-38
Dec. 16	**BALTIMORE**	**W**	**22-16 (OT)**
Dec. 23	at New England	L	7-28
Dec. 30	CINCINNATI	L	25-38

Defensive end Jason Taylor puts his arm around coach Cam Cameron after the team's only win in 2007.
▼

2008

REGULAR SEASON: WON 11, LOST 5
Finished first in AFC East
HEAD COACH: Tony Sparano

H. Wayne Huizenga, in his final year as majority Dolphins owner, brought in future Hall of Famer Bill Parcells to run the team. He fired Cam Cameron and nearly all of the coaching staff. Despite having flimsy head coaching credentials like his predecessor, Tony Sparano was hired by Parcells as coach.

The Dolphins had two great pieces of fortune: Quarterback Chad Pennington was released by the Jets after New York acquired Brett Favre, and the Dolphins benefited from one of the weakest possible schedules, playing teams with a combined winning percentage of .461. That provided the Dolphins with their most recent appearance in the postseason.

Pennington's 97.4 passer rating is the second-best in Dolphins history, behind only Dan Marino's 108.9 from his record-breaking 1984 season.

Date	Opponent	Result	Score
Sept. 7	NEW YORK JETS	L	14-20
Sept. 14	at Arizona	L	10-31
Sept. 21	at New England	W	38-13
Oct. 5	SAN DIEGO	W	17-10
Oct. 12	at Houston	L	28-29
Oct. 19	BALTIMORE	L	13-27
Oct. 26	BUFFALO	W	25-16
Nov. 2	at Denver	W	26-17
Nov. 9	SEATTLE	W	21-19
Nov. 16	OAKLAND	W	17-15
Nov. 23	NEW ENGLAND	L	28-48
Nov. 30	at St. Louis	W	16-12
Dec. 7	Buffalo (in Toronto)	W	16-3
Dec. 14	SAN FRANCISCO	W	14-9
Dec. 21	at Kansas City	W	38-31
Dec. 28	at New York Jets	W	24-17

AFC WILD-CARD PLAYOFF

Date	Opponent	Result	Score
Jan. 4, 2009	BALTIMORE	L	9-27

QB Chad Pennington celebrates a 24-17 victory over the Jets that put the Dolphins into the playoffs.

67

2009

REGULAR SEASON: WON 7, LOST 9
Finished third in AFC East
HEAD COACH: Tony Sparano

Running back Ricky Williams' roller-coaster career in Miami took another upswing as he ran for 1,121 yards, giving him the first-, second- and fifth-highest rushing totals for a season in Dolphins history.

The Dolphins uncovered one of the great late bloomers of all time, plucking LB Cameron Wake from the CFL. In the six years since, Wake has logged 63 sacks and made the Pro Bowl four times.

Steve Ross, who became 50 percent owner of the team in 2008, bought another 45 percent from H. Wayne Huizenga.

The Dolphins were poised to make a run to the post-season when they were 7-6 with two of their three remaining games at home, but they flamed out, going 0-3.

Sept. 13	at Atlanta	L	7-19
Sept. 21	INDIANAPOLIS	L	23-27
Sept. 27	at San Diego	L	13-23
Oct. 4	**BUFFALO**	**W**	**38-10**
Oct. 12	**NEW YORK JETS**	**W**	**31-27**
Oct. 25	NEW ORLEANS	L	34-46
Nov. 1	**at New York Jets**	**W**	**30-25**
Nov. 8	at New England	L	17-27
Nov. 15	**TAMPA BAY**	**W**	**25-23**
Nov. 19	**at Carolina**	**W**	**24-17**
Nov. 29	at Buffalo	L	14-31
Dec. 6	**NEW ENGLAND**	**W**	**22-21**
Dec. 13	**at Jacksonville**	**W**	**14-10**
Dec. 20	at Tennessee	L	24-27 (OT)
Dec. 27	HOUSTON	L	20-27
Jan. 3, 2010	PITTSBURGH	L	24-30

Running back Ricky Williams hurdles over Jaguars safety Reggie Nelson as the Dolphins went on to win 14-10.

2010

REGULAR SEASON: WON 7, LOST 9
Finished third in AFC East
HEAD COACH: Tony Sparano

The Dolphins fired special teams coach John Bonamego after one of the most embarrassing displays by such a unit in a Monday night game in October against New England. The Patriots routed host Miami 41-14, scoring touchdowns on a kickoff return and a blocked field goal and blocking another punt that set up a touchdown.

The 3-2 Dolphins hosted the Pittsburgh Steelers and were victimized by a controversial ending. Trailing 22-20 with less than three minutes left, QB Ben Roethlisberger ran from the 2 and made a dive toward the Miami end zone. Safety Chris Clemons dislodged the ball before the goal line and the fumble went into the end zone, where the Dolphins came up with it. However, the head linesman ruled it a touchdown. The review found that although Roethlisberger fumbled before the goal line, it could not be determined whether the Dolphins clearly recovered. The Steelers retained possession and kicked the winning field goal.

For the second season in a row, the Dolphins, at 7-6, lost their final three games, two of them at home.

Sept. 12	at Buffalo	W	15-10
Sept. 19	**at Minnesota**	**W**	**14-10**
Sept. 26	NEW YORK JETS	L	23-31
Oct. 4	NEW ENGLAND	L	14-41
Oct. 17	**at Green Bay**	**W**	**23-20 (OT)**
Oct. 24	PITTSBURGH	L	22-23
Oct. 31	**at Cincinnati**	**W**	**22-14**
Nov. 7	at Baltimore	L	10-26
Nov. 14	**TENNESSEE**	**W**	**29-17**
Nov. 18	CHICAGO	L	0-16
Nov. 28	**at Oakland**	**W**	**33-17**
Dec. 5	CLEVELAND	L	10-13
Dec. 12	**at New York Jets**	**W**	**10-6**
Dec. 19	BUFFALO	L	14-17
Dec. 26	DETROIT	L	27-34
Jan. 2, 2011	at New England	L	7-38

2011

REGULAR SEASON: WON 6, LOST 10
Finished third in AFC East
HEAD COACH, weeks 1-13: Tony Sparano
HEAD COACH, weeks 14-16: Todd Bowles

The Dolphins got off to an 0-7 start, with the lowlight a game against the Broncos. Miami led 15-0 with less than three minutes left. But a Tim Tebow 5-yard TD pass to Demaryius Thomas with 2:44 left was followed by an onside kick that Denver recovered. Tebow marched his team down the field for a TD with 17 seconds left on a 3-yard pass. With the score 15-13, Tebow ran it in for a two-point conversion. On the Dolphins' second possession of over-time, Matt Moore fumbled on a sack. Denver recovered at the Miami 36. From there, they only managed 2 yards, but it was enough as Matt Prater blasted a 52-yard field goal to sink the Dolphins.

The South Florida community was saddened by the April death of former tight end and beloved Dolphins broadcaster Jim Mandich from bile duct cancer. Mandich made several key catches in the undefeated season of 1972 and had some oft-imitated utterances during his broadcasting career ("Allllllright, Miami!," "Yeahhhhhhhh!!!," "Never better," and "Just driving around with my windows down.")

Coach Tony Sparano was fired with the Dolphins at 4-9. Defensive coordinator Todd Bowles finished the season, going 2-1.

Sept. 12	NEW ENGLAND	L	24-38
Sept. 18	HOUSTON	L	13-23
Sept. 25	at Cleveland	L	16-17
Oct. 2	at San Diego	L	16-26
Oct. 17	at New York Jets	L	6-24
Oct. 23	DENVER	L	15-18 (OT)
Oct. 30	at New York Giants	L	17-20
Nov. 6	at Kansas City	W	31-3
Nov. 13	WASHINGTON	W	20-9
Nov. 20	BUFFALO	W	35-8
Nov. 24	at Dallas	L	19-20
Dec. 4	OAKLAND	W	34-14
Dec. 11	PHILADELPHIA	L	10-26
Dec. 18	at Buffalo	W	30-23
Dec. 24	at New England	L	24-27
Jan. 1, 2012	NEW YORK JETS	W	19-17

Coach Tony Sparano sees things go south in a loss to the Texans.

2012

REGULAR SEASON: WON 7, LOST 9
Finished second in AFC East
HEAD COACH: Joe Philbin

Joe Philbin was hired as Dolphins coach during a wrenching personal crisis. His son Michael drowned in a Wisconsin river on Jan. 8, as interviews were ongoing for the Dolphins coaching position. Philbin was hired less than two weeks later.

Philbin's first season as coach featured a turn on the HBO series "Hard Knocks," where viewers saw the reaction to the arrest and then the release of receiver Chad Ochocinco as the result of a domestic violence incident and the emotional release of cornerback Vontae Davis.

The Dolphins were hobbled by consecutive overtime losses in Weeks 3 and 4, games against the Jets and Cardinals. In each game, they led by more than three points in the fourth quarter.

Sept. 9	at Houston	L	10-30
Sept. 16	OAKLAND	W	35-13
Sept. 23	NEW YORK JETS	L	20-23 (OT)
Sept. 30	at Arizona	L	21-24 (OT)
Oct. 7	at Cincinnati	W	17-13
Oct. 14	ST. LOUIS	W	17-14
Oct. 28	at New York Jets	W	30-9
Nov. 4	at Indianapolis	L	20-23
Nov. 11	TENNESSEE	L	3-37
Nov. 15	at Buffalo	L	14-19
Nov. 25	SEATTLE	W	24-21
Dec. 2	NEW ENGLAND	L	16-23
Dec. 9	at San Francisco	L	13-27
Dec. 16	JACKSONVILLE	W	24-3
Dec. 23	BUFFALO	W	24-10
Dec. 30	at New England	L	0-28

2013

REGULAR SEASON: WON 8, LOST 8
Finished third in AFC East
HEAD COACH: Joe Philbin

The season was swallowed up by the Richie Incognito bullying scandal. In late October, tackle Jonathan Martin left the team facility for good after a prank in the cafeteria. Before long, incendiary texts attributed to Incognito surfaced, and he was suspended. The NFL investigated, and the Ted Wells report stated that there had been a consistent harassment culture and pointed primarily at Incognito, center Mike Pouncey and guard John Jerry. Joe Philbin was also painted as a coach out of touch with his team.

Cameron Wake had one of the NFL's unique plays. His sack for a safety of Andy Dalton occurred in overtime, ending the game against the Bengals.

In 646 dropbacks, Ryan Tannehill was sacked a mind-boggling 58 times, a million miles from Dan Marino's six sacks in 612 dropbacks in 1988. The 58 sacks are tied for the 10th-most times dropped while attempting to pass in an NFL season.

Sept. 8	at Cleveland	W	23-10
Sept. 15	at Indianapolis	W	24-20
Sept. 22	**ATLANTA**	W	27-23
Sept. 30	at New Orleans	L	17-38
Oct. 6	BALTIMORE	L	23-26
Oct. 20	BUFFALO	L	21-23
Oct. 27	at New England	L	17-27
Oct. 31	**CINCINNATI**	W	22-20 (OT)
Nov. 11	at Tampa Bay	L	19-22
Nov. 17	**SAN DIEGO**	W	20-16
Nov. 24	CAROLINA	L	16-20
Dec. 1	**at New York Jets**	W	23-3
Dec. 8	**at Pittsburgh**	W	34-28
Dec. 15	**NEW ENGLAND**	W	24-20
Dec. 22	at Buffalo	L	0-19
Dec. 29	NEW YORK JETS	L	7-20

◀ Quarterback Ryan Tannehill is helped to his feet after being sacked in an exhibition game.

▲
QB Ryan Tannehill looks for a receiver while escaping the pocket in a win over the Bears.

2014

REGULAR SEASON: WON 8, LOST 8
Finished third in AFC East
HEAD COACH: Joe Philbin

Quarterback Ryan Tannehill made a major jump in effectiveness in his third season, pushing his passer rating from 81.7 to 92.8. Only two Miami quarterbacks have had a better number, Dan Marino three times and Chad Pennington in 2008.

The Dolphins traveled to London and defeated the Oakland Raiders 38-14 in Wembley Stadium without the services of pass rusher Dion Jordan, who was suspended for failing a drug test.

The Dolphins made the playoffs once in the past 13 seasons, with two skids of six years without an appearance, interrupted in 2008. Before that, the Dolphins' longest streak without making the postseason had been four seasons.

Sept. 7	NEW ENGLAND	W	33-20
Sept. 14	at Buffalo	L	10-29
Sept. 21	KANSAS CITY	L	15-34
Sept. 28	at Oakland (in London)	W	38-14
Oct. 12	GREEN BAY	L	24-27
Oct. 19	at Chicago	W	27-14
Oct. 26	at Jacksonville	W	27-13
Nov. 2	SAN DIEGO	W	37-0
Nov. 9	at Detroit	L	16-20
Nov. 13	BUFFALO	W	22-9
Nov. 23	at Denver	L	36-39
Dec. 1	at New York Jets	W	16-13
Dec. 7	BALTIMORE	L	13-28
Dec. 14	at New England	L	13-41
Dec. 21	MINNESOTA	W	37-35
Dec. 28	NEW YORK JETS	L	24-37

2015
AND BEYOND

The Dolphins' 50th season starts with a re-stocked team. Miami signed coveted free agent defensive tackle Ndamukong Suh and other free agent veterans such as tight end Jordan Cameron. The Dolphins traded for fleet, young wideout Kenny Stills and drafted wide receiver DeVante Parker (at right) out of Louisville, plus six others. Sun Life Stadium is amid renovations and hopes are high for a renewed on-field product, as well.

Dolphins logo
1989-96

3

THE PLAYERS

TOP 50

PLAYERS IN DOLPHINS HISTORY

BY DAVE HYDE

1

DAN MARINO

{QB // 1983-99} Who else? He rewrote the NFL record books, carried teams with his magical arm, energized a franchise for 17 years and helped turn the Dolphins into a global brand as the the world changed in the 1980s and 1990s.

2

LARRY CSONKA

{FB // 1968-74, '79} The face and the mindset of the Perfect Season. Every Monday meeting would begin with Don Shula reading a scouting report of the upcoming opponent. He'd then ask Csonka what he thought. "F--- the Jets," Csonka would say. Or Bills. Or Patriots. Or whomever.

3

DWIGHT STEPHENSON

{C // 1980-87} The league's dominant offensive lineman of the 1980s. His presence changed the way the offense operated. For instance, his ability to block whomever lined up over him one-on-one was the strategic starting point to the Dolphins' defeat of the famed "46" Bears defense.

4

LARRY LITTLE

{G // 1969-80} Little's five All-Pro selections tie the franchise high. He was involved in the most lopsided trade in franchise history — at least one involving former high school teammates. Mack Lamb was shipped to the Chargers in exchange for Little.

BOB GRIESE

{QB // 1967-80} Griese's leadership, decision-making and sublimated ego were his calling card. He only threw seven passes in the 1974 Super Bowl. Yet by 1977, when that power offense left, he led the league in touchdowns and quarterback rating.

JASON TAYLOR

{LB/DE // 1997-2007, '09, '11} The dominant Dolphins defensive player of his era. An NFL Defensive Player of the Year award. An early Nick Saban comment gives a stellar, yet haunting, description of Taylor's game: "If he'd been in this defense all his career, he'd be in the Hall of Fame." He probably still will.

JIM LANGER

{C // 1970-79} Langer was picked off the waiver wire from Cleveland. He became a starter in 1970 after line coach Monte Clark threatened to resign if he wasn't. He anchored the glory years of the early 1970s.

NICK BUONICONTI

{LB // 1969-76} Spent the first half of his career as a Patriot, so playing eight years as a Dolphin is a handicap in this list. In some ways, he's the Griese of the defense, surrounded by fabulous talent to the point it's hard to gauge his. But he was the centerpiece of the defense.

PAUL WARFIELD

{WR // 1970-74} Can't put him lower than here, even if he only played five Dolphins seasons. They involved three Super Bowl appearances, and his downfield presence became a good reason why. He defined the receiver position in his era.

BOB KUECHENBERG

{OL // 1970-84} How is this man not in the Hall of Fame? With Langer and Little, he was part of the best middle of the line in NFL history. Longevity? He blocked in Super Bowls for Griese and Marino. Talented? He played tackle and guard in 1978, earning postseason awards at each position.

ZACH THOMAS

{LB // 1996-2007} His five All-Pro seasons tie Little as the most in franchise history. The fact they came over an eight-year period shows he played a dominant stretch. For 11 years, he was the perfect fit in a defense built for his athleticism.

MARK CLAYTON

{WR // 1983-92} He was 5-foot-9 of bravado, an eighth-round pick with enough athleticism to dunk a basketball. He hauled in a franchise-record 18 touchdown passes in the magical 1984 season and had at least 10 TDs on four occasions.

BOB BAUMHOWER

{DT // 1977-86} The first of the Killer B's, he was a five-time Pro Bowl player who had 888 tackles and 39 ½ sacks, the most by a tackle in team history.

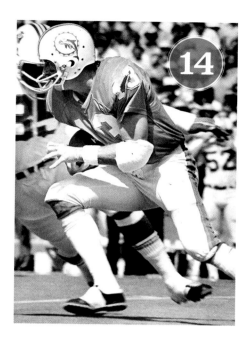

JAKE SCOTT

{S // 1970-75} The franchise's all-time interceptions leader with 35. His interception closed out the Perfect Season Super Bowl, and his combination of macho and intellect stood out in the early 1970s.

DICK ANDERSON

{S // 1968-77} Smart, athletic and fearless, Anderson and Scott were the pair teams couldn't get behind. Anderson is No. 2 in franchise interceptions, with 34.

DOUG BETTERS

{DE // 1978-87} He finished with 43.5 sacks and was selected to the Pro Bowl in 1983 when he made 16 sacks and was NFL Defensive Player of the Year.

RICHMOND WEBB

{LT // 1990-2000} In an era when the left tackle became a marquee position, Webb protected Marino's flank and became his steady, understated bodyguard for a decade of high-scoring Dolphin teams.

BILL STANFILL

{DE // 1969-76} Stretch, as teammates called him, led the franchise with 67 sacks until Jason Taylor passed him. Like most of his early 1970s defensive teammates, injuries kept him from some of the rewards his talent deserved.

JOHN OFFERDAHL

{LB // 1986-93} Five Pro Bowl appearances show he got everything he could from his undersized body to anchor the middle of a 3-4 defense. He was the best player on defense in the late 1980s/early 1990s.

MARK DUPER

{WR // 1982-92} He changed his name legally to "Super Duper" and teamed up with fellow "Marks Brother" Mark Clayton to put up prolific numbers in the Dolphins' high-scoring offense. A favorite target of Dan Marino, Duper's speed spawned the saying, "If he's even, he's leavin'."

MANNY FERNANDEZ

{DL // 1968-75} A force in the middle of the early 1970s. The Washington Redskins' game plan in Super Bowl VII called for running the ball up the middle and blocking Fernandez with a single lineman. He had 17 tackles and a sack in the game.

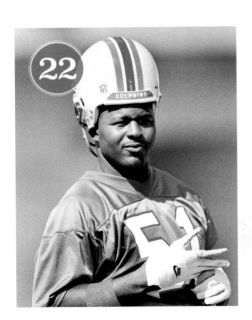

BRYAN COX

{LB // 1991-95} The first picture of Cox as a rookie was wading into the Cincinnati Bengals' sideline to attack a player who had cheap-shotted Pete Stoyanovich. That temperamental image didn't fade through the years.

NAT MOORE

{WR // 1974-86} Moore was solid, smart and consistent enough so that when Marino stumbled in the huddle in calling a play his rookie year, Moore finished the job for him.

JIM KIICK

{RB // 1968-74} Lost in history is how Kiick was named "Butch Cassidy" to Csonka's "Sundance Kid." Early in their careers, Kiick was the more productive player. He led the Dolphins in rushing in 1968 and 1969.

25

MERCURY MORRIS

{RB // 1969-75} He provided the speed to the great 1970s teams and averaged 5.73 yards a carry during the Dolphins' first three Super Bowl years.

26

ED NEWMAN

{G // 1973-84} Former Miami Dolphins guard and current Miami-Dade County Circuit judge was a brick in the Dolphins' line for 12 seasons, getting named to four Pro Bowls. Newman is in the Jewish Sports Hall of Fame.

27

PATRICK SURTAIN

{CB // 1998-2004} The final piece of Jimmy Johnson's fearsome foursome of non-first-round Dolphins picks on defense between '96 and '98. he was a second-rounder and was voted to three Pro Bowls, twice as a starter, in his seven Miami seasons.

28

SAM MADISON

{CB // 1997-2005} Madison was the first Dolphins cornerback ever voted to the Pro Bowl, making four — three as a starter — in his nine years in aqua and orange, despite his well-noted failings in run support.

29

O.J. McDUFFIE

{WR // 1993-2001} Dan Marino called him the "toughest" teammate he ever played with. He led the league in receptions in 1998 and was Marino's best on-field friend for his Dolphins career.

30

CAMERON WAKE

{DE // 2009-14} Wake has been one of the great undrafted finds in team history, coming from the Canadian League and having 63 sacks in his six seasons. He pulled off a rarity in 2013 when he had a walkoff sack for a safety in overtime against the Bengals.

GARO YEPREMIAN

{K // 1970-78} He's remembered for the botched field-goal attempt in the '73 Super Bowl that resulted in him throwing an interception. But his career was full of key moments (a 51-yard field goal against Minnesota to keep the Perfect Season alive) and he was named to the NFL's All-Decade Team of the 1970s.

REGGIE ROBY

{P // 1983-92} "He might have the world's greatest leg," the London Times wrote after watching him punt the length of a soccer field before a Dolphins exhibition game.

TONY NATHAN

{RB // 1979-87} In Dan Marino's first three seasons, Nathan was a star receiving back. He was regularly among team rushing and receiving leaders and delivered a singular moment in the hook-and-lateral play (see p. 137).

BOB MATHESON

{LB // 1971-79} Versatile linebacker who was the number behind the "53" Defense. Matheson joined the Dolphins just in time for their Super Bowl run. He died of Hodgkin's Disease in 1994.

VERN DEN HERDER

{DE // 1971-82} He was the only defensive player to suit up for the Dolphins in four Super Bowls. With 64 sacks, he is in fourth place on the Dolphins' all-time list, one ahead of Cameron Wake.

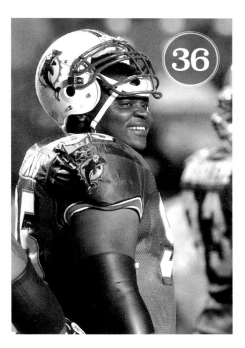

TIM BOWENS

{NT // 1994-2004} A throwback right from his draft workout, when he wore high-top black sneakers and jean shorts, he played 10 solid years, often protecting Zach Thomas from linemen.

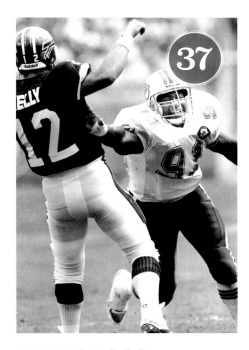

JEFF CROSS

{DE // 1988-95} Cross ranks sixth in franchise history with 59.5 sacks. He made the Pro Bowl in 1990 when he had 11.5 sacks, three forced fumbles and two fumble recoveries.

KIM BOKAMPER

{LB/DE // 1977-85} A nine-year starter and one-time Pro Bowl pick, Bokamper started in two Super Bowls and was an instrumental part of the "Killer B's" defense in the early 1980s.

BOB BRUDZINSKI

{LB // 1981-89} Acquired in a trade from the Rams, Brudzinski was a consistent and solid performer through the 1980s with 14.5 sacks and nine interceptions.

JON GIESLER

{T // 1979-88} Gave 10 good years and two good knees to protecting quarterbacks, centered around the two Super Bowl teams of the 1980s.

KEITH SIMS

{G // 1990-97} Sims, playing alongside Richmond Webb, was part of a vaunted Miami front left side in the 1990s that protected Dan Marino. He was selected to three Pro Bowls, two as a starter.

JIM JENSEN

{WR/RB // 1981-92} Jensen was the Swiss Army Knife of the Dolphins' offense – special-teams stalwart, receiver, running back, even quarterback when needed.

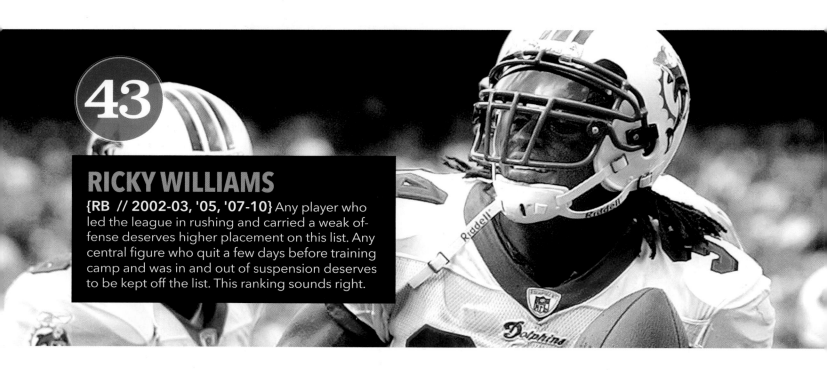

RICKY WILLIAMS

{RB // 2002-03, '05, '07-10} Any player who led the league in rushing and carried a weak offense deserves higher placement on this list. Any central figure who quit a few days before training camp and was in and out of suspension deserves to be kept off the list. This ranking sounds right.

OLINDO MARE

{K // 1997-2006} A local kid who used to jump fences to practice at high school fields, Mare kicked 10 years for the Dolphins. His highlight was kicking an NFL record 39 field goals in 1999.

BRUCE HARDY

{TE // 1978-89} From 1984-86, the athletic Hardy caught 14 of his 25 career touchdown passes from Dan Marino. Hardy went on to coach the defunct Florida Bobcats of the Arena Football League.

46

JIM MANDICH

{TE // 1970-77} Mandich was the "receiving" tight end of the 1970s Dolphins. His late touchdown preserved the Perfect Season in a narrow escape against Minnesota. He became immensely popular as a Dolphins announcer after his retirement as a player. A-L-L-R-I-I-IGHT Miami!!

47

CHAD PENNINGTON

{QB // 2008-10} In 2008, Pennington arrived and showed the value of a great quarterback. After a 1-15 season, Pennington completed a Dolphins-record 67.4 percent of his passes with 19 touchdowns and seven interceptions and led the team to the playoffs.

48

TIM FOLEY

{CB // 1970-80} Remarkably, he was the only Dolphins defensive back to receive Pro Bowl recognition from 1976-98. He wasn't fast – but his mind and football instincts fit that defense perfectly.

49

JEFF DELLENBACH

{OL // 1985-94} Had 10 solid years on the offense at center, guard and tackle. He gained fame for falling on the football that Dallas' Leon Lett mistakenly touched after a blocked field goal in the 1993 Thanksgiving ice bowl.

50

TIM RUDDY

{C // 1994-2003} Undersized for a center, but was a vital part of the Dolphins' line for a decade. For years, coach Jimmy Johnson tried to replace him. He never could find anyone better.

OUR ACCOUNTING OF THE MOST NOTEWORTHY DOLPHINS PLAYERS TO WEAR EACH NUMBER, FROM 1 TO 99.

PRIME NUMBERS

BY STEVE SVEKIS

NO. 99 JASON TAYLOR
DE // 1997-2007, 2009, 2011

NO. 1 GARO YEPREMIAN
K // 1970-78

ORANGE JERSEY
DENOTES MADE
PRO BOWL WITH
DOLPHINS

**GARO
YEPREMIAN**
{K // 1970-78}

**BRANDON
FIELDS**
{K // 2007-14}

**JOEY
HARRINGTON**
{QB // 2006}

**REGGIE
ROBY**
{P // 1983-92}

**UWE VON
SCHAMANN**
{K // 1979-84}

**RAY
LUCAS**
{QB // 2001-02}

**CHAD
HENNE**
{QB // 2008-11}

**DAUNTE
CULPEPPER**
{QB // 2006}

**JAY
FIEDLER**
{QB // 2000-04}

**OLINDO
MARE**
{K // 1997-2006}

**JIM
JENSEN**
{TE // 1981-92}

**BOB
GRIESE**
{QB // 1967-80}

**DAN
MARINO**
{QB // 1983-99}

**JARVIS
LANDRY**
{WR // 2014}

**EARL
MORRALL**
{QB // 1972-76}

**DAVID
WOODLEY**
{QB // 1980-83}

**RYAN
TANNEHILL**
{QB // 2012-14}

**SAGE
ROSENFELS**
{QB // 2002-05}

**BRANDON
MARSHALL**
{WR // 2010-11}

**LARRY
SEIPLE**
{P/WR // 1967-77}

**JIM
KIICK**
{RB // 1968-74}

**MERCURY
MORRIS**
{RB // 1969-75}

**PATRICK
SURTAIN**
{CB // 1998-2004}

**SEAN
SMITH**
{CB // 2009-12}

LOUIS OLIVER
{FS // 1989-93, 1995-96}

LAMAR SMITH
{RB // 2000-01}

LORENZO HAMPTON
{RB // 1985-89}

DON McNEAL
{CB // 1980-89}

SAM MADISON
{CB // 1997-2005}

BERNIE PARMALEE
{RB // 1992-98}

BROCK MARION
{FS // 1998-2003}

JOE AUER
{RB // 1966-67}

SAMMIE SMITH
{RB // 1989-91}

RICKY WILLIAMS
{RB // 2002-03, 2005, 2007-10}

MICHAEL STEWART
{SS // 1994-96}

DON NOTTINGHAM
{FB // 1973-77}

YEREMIAH BELL
{S // 2004-11}

CALVIN JACKSON
{CB/SS // 1994-99}

LARRY CSONKA
{RB // 1968-74, 1979}

DICK ANDERSON
{S // 1968-77}

FULTON WALKER
{KR/DB // 1981-84}

PAUL WARFIELD
{WR // 1970-74}

TERRY KIRBY
{RB // 1993-95}

ROB KONRAD
{FB // 1999-2004}

CURTIS JOHNSON
{CB // 1970-78}

PETE JOHNSON
{FB // 1984}

GLENN BLACKWOOD
{S // 1979-87}

GERALD SMALL
{CB // 1978-83}

WILLIAM JUDSON
{CB // 1981-89}

NO. 44 ROB KONRAD
FB // 1999-2004

95

NO. 56 JOHN OFFERDAHL
LB // 1986-93

OLIVIER VERNON
{DE // 2012-14}

BRYAN COX
{OLB // 1991-95}

CHANNING CROWDER
{LB // 2005-10}

BOB MATHESON
{LB // 1971-79}

ZACH THOMAS
{LB // 1996-2007}

HUGH GREEN
{LB // 1985-91}

JOHN OFFERDAHL
{LB // 1986-93}

DWIGHT STEPHENSON
{C // 1980-87}

KIM BOKAMPER
{DE/LB // 1977-85}

DOUG SWIFT
{LB // 1970-75}

BERT WEIDNER
{OL // 1990-95}

TIM RUDDY
{C // 1994-2003}

JIM LANGER
{C // 1970-79}

MARK DIXON
{LG // 1998-2003}

ED NEWMAN
{G // 1973-84}

JEFF DELLENBACH
{OL // 1985-94}

LARRY LITTLE
{RG // 1969-80}

BOB KUECHENBERG
{LG // 1970-84}

ERIC LAAKSO
{OL // 1978-84}

KEITH SIMS
{LG // 1990-97}

BRIAN SOCHIA
{NT // 1986-91}

BRANDEN ALBERT
{LT // 2014}

VERNON CAREY
{RT // 2004-11}

BOB BAUMHOWER
{DT // 1977-86}

MARK DENNIS
{T // 1987-93}

MANNY FERNANDEZ
{DL // 1968-75}

JAMES BROWN
{T // 1996-99}

A.J. DUHE
{LB // 1977-84}

RICHMOND WEBB
{T // 1990-2000}

JON GIESLER
{T // 1979-88}

JOE ROSE
{TE // 1980-85}

O.J. McDUFFIE
{WR // 1993-2000}

DURIEL HARRIS
{WR // 1976-83, 1985}

MARK CLAYTON
{WR // 1983-92}

BILL STANFILL
{DE // 1969-76}

NICK BUONICONTI
{LB // 1969-76}

ORONDE GADSDEN
{WR // 1998-2003}

YATIL GREEN
{WR // 1997-99}

JIM MANDICH
{TE // 1970-77}

NAT MOORE
{WR // 1974-86}

ERIC KUMEROW
{DE // 1988-90}

CAMERON WAKE
{DE // 2009-14}

DARYL GARDENER
{DT // 1996-2001}

TRACE ARMSTRONG
{DE // 1995-2000}

RANDY STARKS
{DL // 2008-14}

TIM BOWENS
{DT // 1994-2004}

ALFRED OGLESBY
{DL // 1990-92}

JOHN BOSA
{DE // 1987-89}

JARED ODRICK
{DT // 2010-14}

JASON TAYLOR
{DE // 1997-2007, 2009, 2011}

NO. 95 TIM BOWENS
DT // 1994-2004

ALL-TIME TEAMS

After you write in Dan Marino as quarterback, how do you decide which of the hundreds of players over 49 seasons would make the ultimate Dolphins team? Our panel of former players and journalists made their picks.

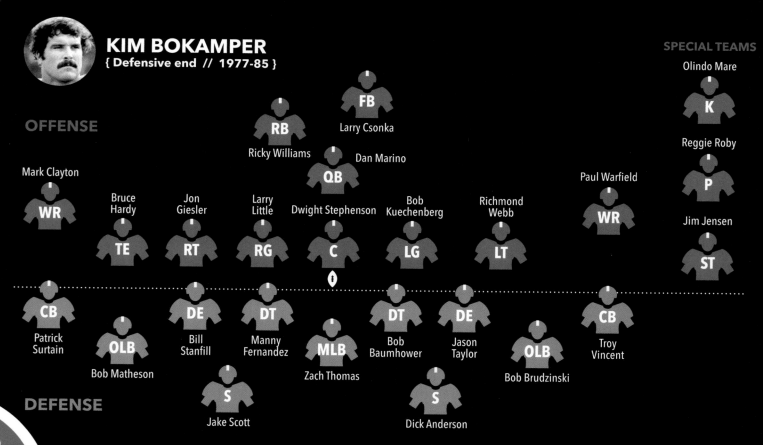

KIM BOKAMPER
{ Defensive end // 1977-85 }

SPECIAL TEAMS

Olindo Mare — K

Reggie Roby — P

Jim Jensen — ST

OFFENSE

- FB — Larry Csonka
- RB — Ricky Williams
- QB — Dan Marino
- Mark Clayton — WR
- TE — Bruce Hardy
- RT — Jon Giesler
- RG — Larry Little
- C — Dwight Stephenson
- LG — Bob Kuechenberg
- LT — Richmond Webb
- Paul Warfield — WR

DEFENSE

- CB — Patrick Surtain
- OLB — Bob Matheson
- DE — Bill Stanfill
- DT — Manny Fernandez
- MLB — Zach Thomas
- DT — Bob Baumhower
- DE — Jason Taylor
- OLB — Bob Brudzinski
- CB — Troy Vincent
- S — Jake Scott
- S — Dick Anderson

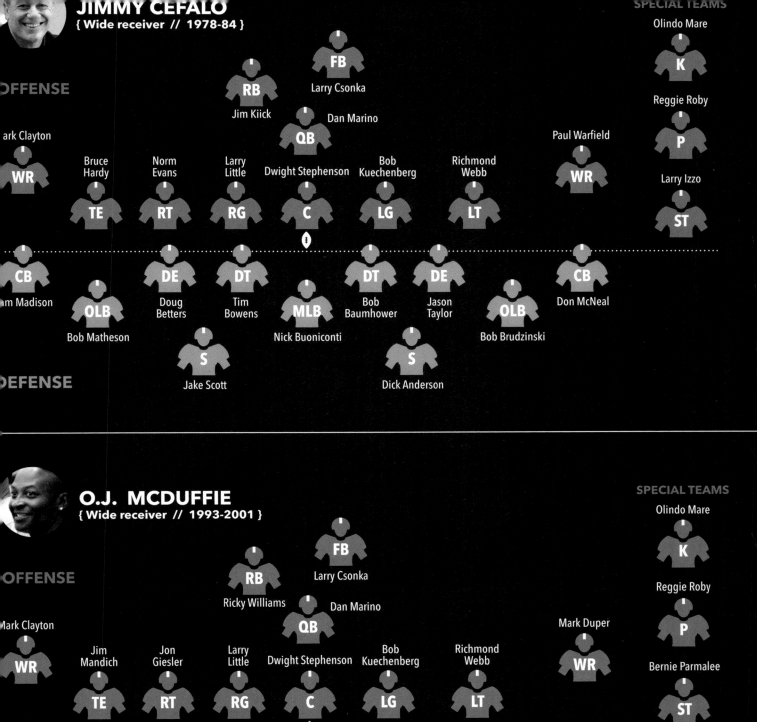

JIMMY CEFALO
{ Wide receiver // 1978-84 }

OFFENSE

SPECIAL TEAMS

- FB — Larry Csonka
- RB — Jim Kiick
- QB — Dan Marino
- WR — ark Clayton
- TE — Bruce Hardy
- RT — Norm Evans
- RG — Larry Little
- C — Dwight Stephenson
- LG — Bob Kuechenberg
- LT — Richmond Webb
- WR — Paul Warfield
- K — Olindo Mare
- P — Reggie Roby
- ST — Larry Izzo

DEFENSE

- CB — m Madison
- OLB — Bob Matheson
- DE — Doug Betters
- DT — Tim Bowens
- MLB — Nick Buoniconti
- DT — Bob Baumhower
- DE — Jason Taylor
- OLB — Bob Brudzinski
- CB — Don McNeal
- S — Jake Scott
- S — Dick Anderson

O.J. MCDUFFIE
{ Wide receiver // 1993-2001 }

OFFENSE

SPECIAL TEAMS

- FB — Larry Csonka
- RB — Ricky Williams
- QB — Dan Marino
- WR — Mark Clayton
- TE — Jim Mandich
- RT — Jon Giesler
- RG — Larry Little
- C — Dwight Stephenson
- LG — Bob Kuechenberg
- LT — Richmond Webb
- WR — Mark Duper
- K — Olindo Mare
- P — Reggie Roby
- ST — Bernie Parmalee

DEFENSE

- CB — Patrick Surtain
- OLB — Bryan Cox
- DE — Doug Betters
- DT — Manny Fernandez
- MLB — Zach Thomas
- DT — Tim Bowens
- DE — Jason Taylor
- OLB — Bob Brudzinski
- CB — Troy Vincent
- S — Jake Scott
- S — Dick Anderson

DAVE HYDE
{ Columnist // Sun Sentinel }

OFFENSE

- FB — Larry Csonka
- RB — Ricky Williams
- QB — Dan Marino
- WR — Mark Clayton
- TE — Jim Mandich
- RT — Norm Evans
- RG — Larry Little
- C — Dwight Stephenson
- LG — Bob Kuechenberg
- LT — Richmond Webb
- WR — Paul Warfield

Garo Yepre—
K

Reggie R—
P

Jim Jens—
ST

DEFENSE

- CB — Patrick Surtain
- OLB — Bryan Cox
- DE — Bill Stanfill
- DT — Manny Fernandez
- MLB — Nick Buoniconti
- DT — Bob Baumhower
- DE — Jason Taylor
- OLB — Bob Brudzinski
- CB — Sam Madison
- S — Jake Scott
- S — Dick Anderson

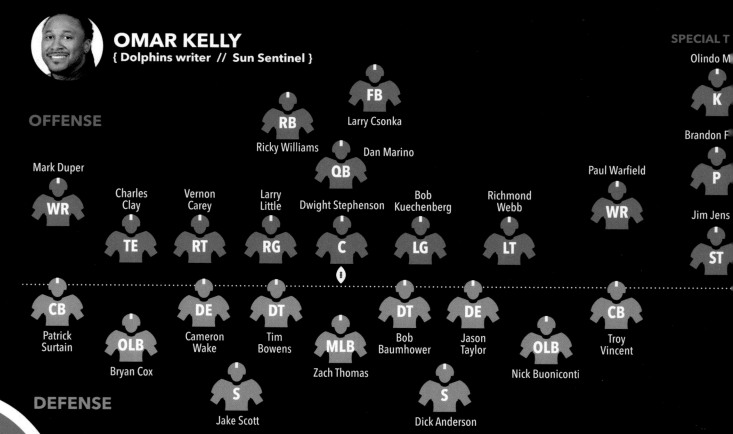

OMAR KELLY
{ Dolphins writer // Sun Sentinel }

OFFENSE

- FB — Larry Csonka
- RB — Ricky Williams
- QB — Dan Marino
- WR — Mark Duper
- TE — Charles Clay
- RT — Vernon Carey
- RG — Larry Little
- C — Dwight Stephenson
- LG — Bob Kuechenberg
- LT — Richmond Webb
- WR — Paul Warfield

SPECIAL T

Olindo M—
K

Brandon F—
P

Jim Jens—
ST

DEFENSE

- CB — Patrick Surtain
- OLB — Bryan Cox
- DE — Cameron Wake
- DT — Tim Bowens
- MLB — Zach Thomas
- DT — Bob Baumhower
- DE — Jason Taylor
- OLB — Nick Buoniconti
- CB — Troy Vincent
- S — Jake Scott
- S — Dick Anderson

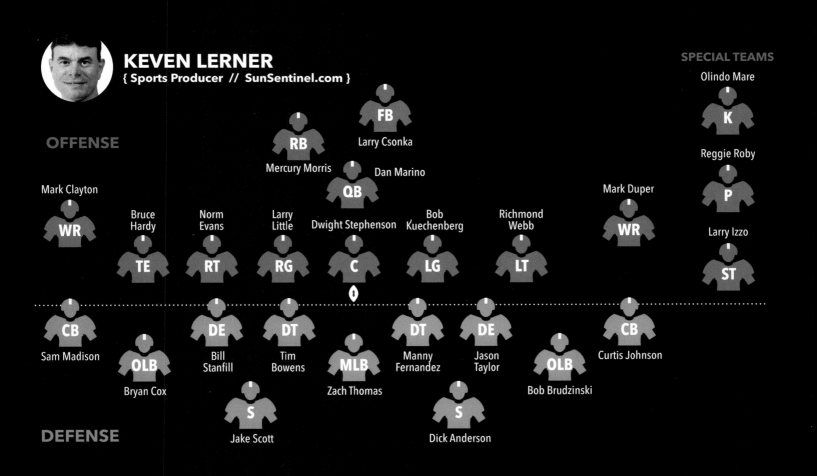

KEVEN LERNER
{ Sports Producer // SunSentinel.com }

OFFENSE

SPECIAL TEAMS

Larry Csonka — FB
Mercury Morris — RB
Dan Marino — QB
Mark Clayton — WR
Bruce Hardy — TE
Norm Evans — RT
Larry Little — RG
Dwight Stephenson — C
Bob Kuechenberg — LG
Richmond Webb — LT
Mark Duper — WR

Olindo Mare — K
Reggie Roby — P
Larry Izzo — ST

DEFENSE

Sam Madison — CB
Bryan Cox — OLB
Bill Stanfill — DE
Tim Bowens — DT
Zach Thomas — MLB
Manny Fernandez — DT
Jason Taylor — DE
Bob Brudzinski — OLB
Curtis Johnson — CB
Jake Scott — S
Dick Anderson — S

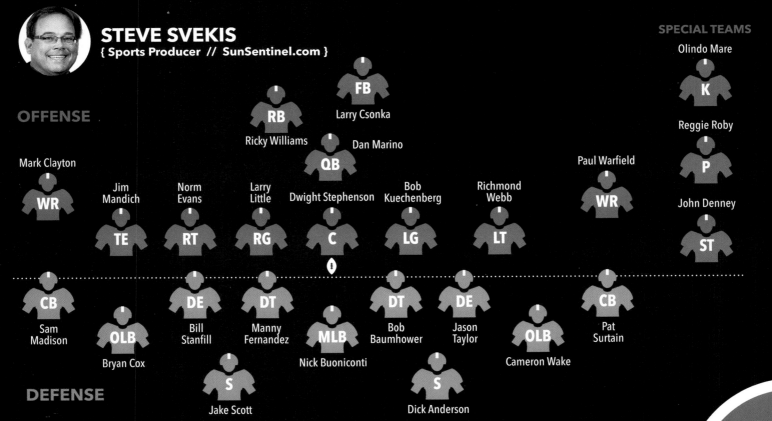

STEVE SVEKIS
{ Sports Producer // SunSentinel.com }

OFFENSE

SPECIAL TEAMS

Larry Csonka — FB
Ricky Williams — RB
Dan Marino — QB
Mark Clayton — WR
Jim Mandich — TE
Norm Evans — RT
Larry Little — RG
Dwight Stephenson — C
Bob Kuechenberg — LG
Richmond Webb — LT
Paul Warfield — WR

Olindo Mare — K
Reggie Roby — P
John Denney — ST

DEFENSE

Sam Madison — CB
Bryan Cox — OLB
Bill Stanfill — DE
Manny Fernandez — DT
Nick Buoniconti — MLB
Bob Baumhower — DT
Jason Taylor — DE
Cameron Wake — OLB
Pat Surtain — CB
Jake Scott — S
Dick Anderson — S

GREATEST DRAFT PICKS & GREATEST DRAFT BUSTS*

(*ONLY INCLUDES TOP-50 PICKS)

FROM HIDDEN GEMS TO REGRETFUL PICKS, OMAR KELLY (HITS) **AND STEVE SVEKIS** (MISSES) **RANK THE DOLPHINS' HISTORY IN THE DRAFT.**

QB DAN MARINO
{1983 // 1st round, No. 27}

Five quarterbacks were selected in the 1983 draft, one of the better quarterback classes in NFL history. Three of those quarterbacks are in the Hall of Fame, and Marino's the one who holds the most records. His 61,361 yards passing ranks third on the NFL's all-time career passing list, and he was selected to nine Pro Bowls. Because of Marino, the Dolphins didn't need to address the quarterback position for two decades.

C DWIGHT STEPHENSON
{1980 // 2nd round, No. 48}

Stephenson played his entire Hall of Fame career with the Dolphins and was hailed by some as the best to ever play his position. Stephenson anchored an offensive line that allowed the fewest sacks in the NFL each of his seven seasons. His playing career ended after he tore two knee ligaments against the Jets on Dec. 7, 1987, when he was hit by Marty Lyons on a Jets fumble return.

HITS

1

2

MISSES

DE DION JORDAN
{2013 // 1st round, No. 3}

Before burning the third pick on the pass rusher from Oregon, the Dolphins tossed the 12th and 42nd picks to Oakland. Things were weird right out of the gate. Jordan missed team practices because of his school's quarter system. Then came the lack of production (for every forced fumble came multiple games of on-field anonymity). Then, in 2014, NFL drug suspensions cost him eight games. In 2015, a seasonlong suspension.

DB JAMAR FLETCHER
{2001 // 1st round, No. 26}

The Dolphins had a chance to select a quarterback who would have spectacularly followed Dan Marino. However, they selected Wisconsin's Fletcher and allowed Drew Brees to be gobbled up by San Diego six selections later. Fletcher had two interceptions in three seasons, Brees went on to break Marino's single-season passing yardage record as part of a sure Hall of Fame career.

FB LARRY CSONKA
{1968 // 1st round, No. 8}
Csonka, a star from Syracuse, became the Dolphins' all-time leading rusher, gaining 6,737 yards and scoring 53 touchdowns on 1,506 carries. The five-time Pro Bowl pick had three consecutive 1,000-yard seasons (1971-73) while sharing the backfield with Mercury Morris. He retired after the 1979 season ranked fifth in NFL history for most rushing attempts and sixth for most rushing yards and rushing touchdowns.

QB BOB GRIESE
{1967 // 1st round, No. 4}
Any time a drafted player makes it to the Hall of Fame after playing his entire career with one team, that franchise made a great pick. Griese, a Purdue product, threw for more than 25,000 yards and scored 192 touchdowns for the Dolphins. Including the playoffs, Griese had a .681 winning percentage (88-41-1) and made six appearances in the Pro Bowl.

HITS
3

4
MISSES

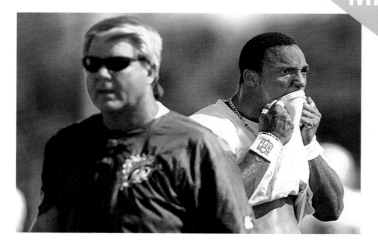

RB JOHN AVERY
{1998 // 1st round, No. 29}
If the heights of Jimmy Johnson's renowned draft doings came in Dallas when he maneuvered up for Emmitt Smith, perhaps his biggest wheeling-and-dealing mistake was in 1998 when he traded down from 19th to 29th. Randy Moss was selected 21st by Minnesota and had a Hall of Fame career. But Avery never made sense. Undersized and without quickness, he flamed out quickly and was gone from Miami after 17 games.

DE ERIC KUMEROW
{1988 // 1st round, No. 16}
The Kumerow selection was met with a resounding chorus of "Who?" The Ohio State defensive end was a non-impact player with five sacks over his three seasons in South Florida, and he headed up the last of five disastrous drafts after the team's Super Bowl XIX appearance. The ineptitude paved the way for Miami to endure five seasons with eight wins or fewer from 1986-91.

LB **ZACH THOMAS**
{1996 // 5th round, No. 154}

Zach Thomas became the first of Jimmy Johnson's many draft gems during his tenure as the Dolphins' coach and top executive. The former Texas Tech standout became an immediate starter and spent 12 seasons as the anchor of the Dolphins' defense. Thomas was a seven-time Pro Bowl selection and was named to the NFL's 2000s All-Decade team.

DE **JASON TAYLOR**
{1997 // 3rd round, No. 73}

The Dolphins drafted this two-sport athlete from the University of Akron with hopes he would become a solid pro. Fortunately for Miami, Taylor turned into a six-time Pro Bowl selection who was named to the NFL's 2000s All-Decade team. Taylor produced 139.5 sacks, forced 40 fumbles and intercepted eight passes in his 15-year NFL career (13 with the Dolphins). He is sixth all-time in career sacks.

HITS 5

6 MISSES

WR **YATIL GREEN**
{1997 // 1st round, No. 15}

Jimmy Johnson wanted to get aging QB Dan Marino some outside wideout speed to pair up with first-down machine O.J. McDuffie, so he went to down to Coral Gables to pick Green, who had had nagging injuries at the University of Miami but nothing serious. In the first practice of training camp, Green blew out his knee. He then did it again the next season.

RB **SAMMIE SMITH**
{1989 // 1st round, No. 9}

The former FSU star became known for his fumble-itis, putting more balls on the ground (17) than into the end zone (16) in his three seasons. Further, he had a paltry 3.5 yards per carry. It was Miami's first top-10 draft pick in the coach Don Shula era and the beginning of a spotty franchise record of picking in the top third of the first round (Ronnie Brown, Ted Ginn Jr., Jake Long, Dion Jordan).

S JAKE SCOTT
{1970 // 7th round, No. 159}

This former Georgia standout went to five consecutive Pro Bowls during his six-year career with the Dolphins. He was a key member of the 1972 undefeated Dolphins and finished that season as MVP of Super Bowl VII, recording two interceptions and 63 return yards in the Dolphins' 14-7 win. Scott had 35 interceptions in his six seasons, which makes him the Dolphins' all-time leader in that category.

LB BRYAN COX
{1991 // 5th round, No. 113}

The fifth-round pick from Western Illinois became the best in the Dolphins' 1991 draft class. The bombastic and talented Cox often stirred things up in his 12-year career that began with five seasons in Miami. He was named to the Pro Bowl three times while with the Dolphins. He won a Super Bowl with New England, just one of the five teams he played for.

HITS **7**

MISSES **8**

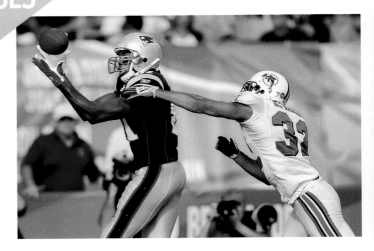

WR TED GINN JR.
{2007 // 1st round, No. 9}

Coach Cam Cameron, in his one ill-fated Dolphins season, had a tenure peppered with awkward spoken moments, most notably his utterance about how the Dolphins had drafted "the entire Ginn family." Although Ginn was a gifted return man, he never could use his speed and elusiveness to get open. The Dolphins compounded the error with the waste of a 40th pick on incapable quarterback John Beck.

CB JASON ALLEN
{2006 // 1st round, No. 16}

Coach Nick Saban's success against the SEC never translated into success for his regime's high draft picks from his former conference opponents. Former Tennessee Volunteer Allen was repeatedly beaten over the top (and on many other routes) by NFL receivers.

WR **MARK CLAYTON**
{1983 // 8th round, No. 223}

Dan Marino wasn't the only gem the Dolphins found in the 1983 draft. That class also featured a Louisville receiver named Mark Clayton, who finished his 11-year NFL career with 582 receptions for 8,974 yards, along with 108 rushing yards, 40 kickoff-return yards and 485 punt-return yards. He also scored 88 touchdowns (87 receiving and 1 punt return).

OT **RICHMOND WEBB**
{1990 // 1st round, No. 9}

Webb, a former Texas A&M standout, protected Dan Marino's blindside for 11 seasons and started 118 consecutive games, second most in team history. Webb and Keith Sims, who was selected in the second round of the same draft, anchored the Dolphins' offensive line for a decade. Webb was a seven-time Pro Bowl selection and a member of the NFL's 1990s All-Decade Team.

HITS

9

10

MISSES

T **BILLY MILNER**
{1995 // 1st round, No. 25}

More of a tandem debacle, the Milner-Andrew Greene draft attempted to replicate the 1990 Richmond Webb-Keith Sims draft. However, 1995 was an unmitigated disaster, with Milner gone from Miami after four games of his second season and the guard Greene – selected 53rd – gone after one season. Never has a tandem of Dolphins draft picks from the first two rounds spent such little time in Miami.

LB **JACKIE SHIPP**
{1984 // 1st round, No. 14}

The Dolphins hadn't had a flameout with their top pick in Don Shula's 14 seasons, but the former Oklahoma Sooner was the first of a series of misfires. The Dolphins' defense, which had allowed 17.2 points a game in the 1980s, fell back to 23.0 a game from 1985-89. The whole 1984 draft was a disaster, with the 12 selections playing for measly 16 seasons combined.

CALL
TO THE
HALL

**NINE LEGENDS HAVE CEMENTED THEIR PLACES
IN NFL HISTORY WITH A SPOT IN CANTON.**
BY CHRIS PERKINS

DON SHULA

{COACH // 1970-95}

A no-nonsense leader, Shula's 347 career victories make him the winningest coach in NFL history, and he has a career record of 347-173-6 (.665). Among his many notable achievements was coaching the 1972 Dolphins to a 17-0 record in the Perfect Season. They're the only team to have an undefeated regular season and win the Super Bowl. Shula, in fact, won Super Bowls VII and VIII (1972-73 seasons), making him one of six coaches to win consecutive Super Bowls. He's also one of three coaches to advance to three consecutive Super Bowls (VI, VII, VIII). He was unanimously elected to the Hall of Fame in 1997, his first year of eligibility.

DWIGHT STEPHENSON

{CENTER // 1980-87}

Widely considered the best center in the NFL during his career, Stephenson was a staple on the offensive line that made quarterback Dan Marino one of the least-sacked quarterbacks in the league during the early part of his career. Stephenson was named All Pro five consecutive years (1983-87) and selected for the Pro Bowl during that same stretch. His career was ended by a December 1987 knee injury. A quick and explosive lineman, Stephenson played in two Super Bowls (XVII and XIX). He was elected to the Hall of Fame in 1998.

LARRY CSONKA
{RUNNING BACK // 1968-74, 79}

The hard-running Csonka was one of the NFL's most-feared offensive players during his career. He rushed for more than 1,000 yards each season during the Dolphins' three-year Super Bowl stretch (Super Bowls VI-VIII). Csonka, a five-time Pro Bowl selection, is the franchise's all-time leading rusher with 6,737 yards during his two stints with the team. "Zonk" was the MVP of Super Bowl VIII after rushing for 145 yards and two touchdowns. Csonka, who played for Memphis of the World Football League (1975) and the New York Giants from 1976-78, averaged a bruising 4.5 yards per carry during his years with the Dolphins. He was elected to the Hall of Fame in 1987, his second year of eligibility.

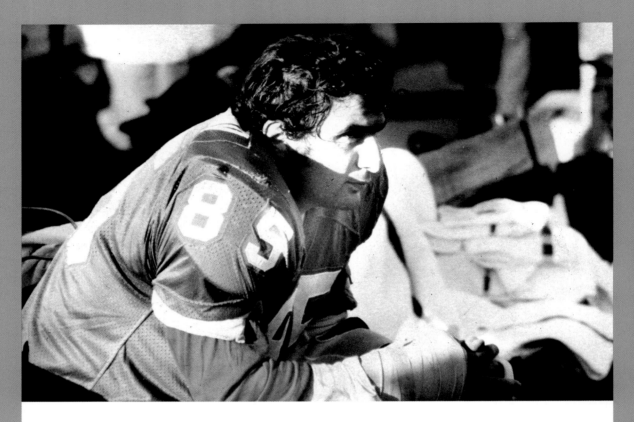

NICK BUONICONTI

{LINEBACKER // 1969-76}

———

At 5-foot-11, 220 pounds, he was a fierce competitor and a leader on the famous "No-Name Defense." He's the Dolphins' only defensive player in the Hall of Fame. Buoniconti played seven seasons for the Dolphins and advanced to three Super Bowls (VI, VII, VIII), winning two (VII, VIII). He played a total of 14 seasons for the Dolphins and Boston Patriots (1962-76). Buoniconti was named to the All-Time AFL team and was named first team All AFL/AFC eight times. He was elected to the Hall of Fame in 2001.

JIM LANGER

{CENTER // 1970-79}

———

Langer, undrafted out of South Dakota State, developed into a mainstay on a highly productive offensive line that cleared the way for Hall of Fame running back Larry Csonka and provided protection for two other future Hall of Famers: QB Bob Griese and WR Paul Warfield. Langer was a five-time All-Pro and six-time Pro Bowl selection and was named team MVP in 1975. He played every offensive snap of the 1972 Perfect Season. He was elected to the Hall of Fame in 1987, his first year of eligibility.

BOB GRIESE

{QUARTERBACK // 1967-80}

The cerebral Griese, who late in his career became known for wearing eyeglasses during games, was the consummate winner, achieving an 88-41-1 record (.681). The six-time Pro Bowl selection led the Dolphins to three consecutive Super Bowls (VI, VII and VIII). In the undefeated 1972 season, Griese sustained a broken leg and dislocated ankle early in the season and returned during the playoffs to lead the Dolphins to the title. Griese passed for 25,092 yards, 192 touchdowns and 172 interceptions during his 14-year career, all with the Dolphins. He was elected to the Hall of Fame in 1990.

LARRY LITTLE

{GUARD // 1969-80}

W hen the Dolphins went to their bread-and-butter running game, it was often Little leading the way as the pulling guard on a sweep. Little, undrafted out of Bethune-Cookman, signed with San Diego and spent his first two seasons with the Chargers. He was traded to the Dolphins in 1969 and became a steadying force at right guard, being named All-Pro six times. Little and Jim Langer, the Hall of Fame center, combined to blow open holes for one of the NFL's best running games, powered largely by Larry Csonka. Little was among the group that led the Dolphins to three consecutive Super Bowls (VI, VII and VIII). He was elected to the Hall of Fame in 1993.

PAUL WARFIELD

{WIDE RECEIVER // 1970-74}

Although he only played five seasons with the Dolphins, Warfield electrified the offense with his big-play skills. He averaged 21.5 yards per reception (156 receptions for 3,355 yards) and had 33 touchdowns. He led the franchise in receiving yards and receiving touchdowns when he left, and his 21.5 yards per catch remains a franchise record. Warfield was a five-time Pro Bowl selection during his five-year Dolphins career and helped win two Super Bowls (VII and VIII). Warfield played for Cleveland (1964-69), Miami (1970-74), Memphis (1975) and Cleveland (1976-77). He was elected to the Hall of Fame in 1982.

DAN MARINO

{QUARTERBACK // 1983-99}

Arguably the best passer in NFL history, Marino's 61,361 passing yards were No. 1 in NFL history when he retired after the 1999 season, as were his 420 touchdown passes. He was the first quarterback to pass for more than 5,000 yards in a season (5,084) in 1984, his second year in the league. His 48 touchdown passes that year were also a record. Marino, known for his quick release and ability to rack up major yards, was a nine-time Pro Bowl selection and eight-time All Pro in his 17-year career, all with the Dolphins. His 13 games of 400 or more yards passing is an NFL record. Marino did much of his damage with wide receivers Mark Clayton and Mark Duper. Marino appeared in one Super Bowl (XIX). He was elected to the Hall of Fame in 2005, his first year of eligibility.

Dolphins logo
1997-2012

4

THE COACHES

{COACH: 1970-95 // RECORD: 274-147-2}

DON SHULA

History began with a hiccup. The first phone call Don Shula received about the Dolphins job came from a college friend, Bill Braucher, a Miami sports writer who was serving as team owner Joe Robbie's icebreaking proxy. Shula interrupted Braucher's greeting with four hurried words from his Baltimore home.

"I've got to go …" Shula said.

He hung up the phone.

Two of his Baltimore assistant coaches were in a fistfight in his front yard. Shula ran out the door and, in a signature of everything to come, waded right into the middle of the fight, began delivering instructions and broke up the fight. A thousand moments came to define Shula over the next 27 years with the Dolphins: He told a referee who pooh-poohed a 5-yard, preseason penalty, "Five yards is my life!" He ran four-a-day practices in his first training camp. He was praised by coaching peer and cowboy Bum Phillips: "He can take his'n and beat your'n or your'n and beat his'n." He invented the platoon system to much ridicule as a way to alternate the disparate talents of running backs Jim Kiick and Mercury Morris. He coached the NFL's only perfect season.

He went to Super Bowls with Earl Morrall (in Baltimore), Bob Griese, Dan Marino and, yes, David Woodley at quarterback. He changed from a power-running coach in the 1970s to a revolutionary passing coach in the 1980s. He survived 33 consecutive seasons in a sport that invented coaching burnout. He won a transcendent 347 games, the most in NFL history.

Perhaps that first phone call from the Dolphins told them who they would hire, though. For the next 26 years with the Dolphins, that's how he approached every work day, getting in the mix, directly confronting problems and leading by strong way of example. Greatness, he felt, was defined in things great and small. You either worked the right way or for another team. Once, early in his Dolphins' tenure, he yelled at fullback Larry Csonka from across the practice field.

"Csonka! What the hell are you doing?" he said.

Csonka, lining up at fullback, froze and looked around. What was wrong?

"You're lined up a step too wide!" Shula said.

Everyone looked. He was a step too wide.

"If a linebacker was coming, you couldn't have blocked him!" Shula yelled.

That was Shula at his best. It's how he approached every work day. He made no pretense of seeing a world bigger than 100 yards long, the way others do as fame and celebrity beckon. Everything was heard through a filter of football. After hearing a visitor Robbie invited into a postgame locker room was a writer — "A writer!" Shula yelled — he threw famous author James Michener out into the cold. He was introduced after a game in the locker room to "Miami Vice" actors Don Johnson and Philip Michael Thomas during their heyday in the 1980s. He actually thought they were police detectives. He thanked them for the work they performed. Miami Vice? What's that?

What he did, Sunday after Sunday, season after season, was put his body of work on display. What a constantly changing, wonderfully talented body of work it became, too. When offensive muscle was the strength of his roster, Csonka became the face of the franchise. When a dominant defense took over, he won with the Killer B's and by managing Woodley. When Marino came aboard in 1983, he ripped up the playbook and rewrote the record books with a passing offense. So many greats are rooted in their time like a period piece. Shula's greatness is he bridged several generations, from a running NFL to a passing one, from the small-money NFL to the highly corporate NFL, from the high-top shoes of John Unitas to the Zubaz pants of Marino.

All the stats and snippets tell how Shula applied his full intelligence and talent toward one focused but immeasurable goal: becoming the best coach football ever had. And he was by the one defining measurement.

"How do you decide the winner in games?" he'd always ask when someone wondered how to measure coaches.

"By the scoreboard," the answer typically came.

He'd say nothing. He'd let that marinate. He knew where 347 wins ranked on the scoreboard. His name is a steakhouse and an expressway to tomorrow's generations. But no one roamed a sideline like him. No one won like him. No one defined who a football coach was, jaw jutting, mind whirling, quite like Don Shula.

— DAVE HYDE

Opposite page, from left: QB Dan Marino talks with coach Don Shula as backup Scott Secules listens during a 1989 game; Shula gives an earful to the side judge at the Super Bowl in 1983; Shula is carried off the field after beating the Eagles in 1993 for his record 325th coaching victory. This page, Shula poses in 2006 with a replica of the Super Bowl VII trophy.

{COACH: 1966-69 // RECORD: 15-39-2}

GEORGE WILSON

An old-school guy who had a hard-living character, Wilson was a veteran NFL coach with the personality to help market an expansion team. He set the mood for the team of castoffs, which included his namesake son, George Wilson Jr., as a backup quarterback. That could be seen by the coach celebrating the franchise-opening win by starting his news conference by throwing a winning fist into the air. It also could be seen by the manner in which he conducted the team. After a preseason game in Jacksonville, he stopped the team bus driving back to Miami and bought drinks for all the players. At lunch, he'd take his staff down the road from the practice facility to Johnny Raffa's restaurant and return with alcohol on his breath. "A floating cocktail party," Nick Buoniconti called the team flights to games. They didn't win much. But they had as much fun as any team that didn't win.

{COACH: 1996-99 //
RECORD: 38-31}

JIMMY JOHNSON

Johnson replaced Don Shula, vamped the roster, reconstructed e salary-cap situation in a healthy nner, drafted four All-Pro play- s and went to three playoffs in ir years, winning two postseason mes. Those accomplishments uld brand a lesser name a suc- ss. In the four seasons before s arrival, the Dolphins had won st one playoff game. But John- n entered with a bold vision of creating his Super Bowl success m Dallas. His inability to match s own expectations led to disap- intment. His clash with Dan arino near the end of the fran- ise quarterback's career split the base. His attempt to quit after third season, when his mother's ath caused a change in perspec- e, led to a troubled fourth season at won a playoff game in Seattle fore ending his reign with a 62-7 ss in Jacksonville. Johnson left e team in good standing, as a fense with a young Jason Taylor, ch Thomas, Patrick Surtain and m Madison gave the franchise a ong foundation for years.

129

{COACH: 2000-04 // RECORD: 43-33}

DAVE WANNSTEDT

Wannstedt spent a year on Jimmy Johnson's coaching staff to smooth a takeover as head coach. The first season was smooth, too. The Dolphins won the AFC East, beat the Colts in overtime in the playoffs and appeared to be on their way under Wannstedt's direction. That turned out to be the best season of his five years. His time became defined not just by disappointments on the field. On the day before the 2001 draft, head of college scouting Tom Braatz pleaded with Wannstedt to draft quarterback Drew Brees over cornerback Jamar Fletcher. Wannstedt chose Fletcher, who played three uneventful seasons for the team. Brees later led New Orleans to a Super Bowl title. It was on such decisions the Wannstedt era turned. He picked little-used linebacker Eddie Moore over future All-Pro receiver Anquan Boldin. He traded for Ricky Williams, then ran him a league-high 383 and 392 times in two seasons. Williams quit before the 2004 season, in part for fear of his body breaking down. In a final hope for success, team owner H. Wayne Huizenga took the personnel decisions from Wannstedt before the 2004 season and gave them to General Manager Rick Spielman. But that just translated into more wasted draft picks. Wannstedt resigned with the team at 1-8 during the 2004 season. Jim Bates was named interim coach to finish the season.

NICK SABAN

Owner H. Wayne Huizenga was known for closing deals, and convincing the sought-after Saban to leave the college ranks where he was king was evidence of that. When Saban went 9-7 and closed his first season with a six-game win streak, big expectations followed him into the next year. Sports Illustrated picked the Dolphins to make the Super Bowl. But in a fateful decision based on medical advice, Saban chose quarterback Daunte Culpepper, who was recovering from a knee injury, rather than Drew Brees, who had a shoulder injury. Culpepper never became the quarterback for the Dolphins that Brees was for the Saints. When Saban went 6-10 his second season, another Dolphins regime became defined by passing on Brees. Saban, too, became defined by a quirky personality. Some players pointed to Saban stepping over a convulsing Jeno James in the locker room after practice. Others to Saban getting ruffled when an equipment manager greeted him as they arrived for work in the morning. Ultimately, though, the personal decisions led to the ultimate personality quirk in Saban: Two weeks after saying, "I won't be the Alabama coach," he abandoned his contract and took the job as Alabama's coach.

{COACH: 2007 // RECORD: 1-15}

CAM CAMERON

Cameron had just five years' experience as a head coach at Indiana University before being named the Dolphins coach. He littered the air with unusual sayings and decisions: "We drafted Ted Ginn and his family," he said on draft day. "We want to fail forward fast," he said of his philosophy. He repeatedly stressed that character would be a deciding factor on his team, but a week after signing high-priced free agent Joey Porter, the linebacker got into a fight in Las Vegas. A coach out of his element combined with a rebuilding team, and the Dolphins threatened to become the second winless team in NFL history. Several veterans spoke out against Cameron's tactics. At 0-13, they beat Baltimore in overtime for the lone win of the season That was perhaps the only good day of Cameron's one year. Bill Parcells was hired near the end of that season to be the football czar, and his first major move after that season was to fire Cameron.

131

{COACH: 2008-11 // RECORD: 29-33}

TONY SPARANO

A tough, direct-talking football lifer, Sparano got the chance he was waiting for when he was hired as Dolphins coach by his mentor, Bill Parcells. When his team started 0-2, he huddled with his coaches on a flight back from Arizona. "We've got to do something," he said. The next week, Sparano sprung "The Wildcat" formation on Bill Belichick and the Patriots in Foxborough, and it sparked a brilliant 38-13 win against the perennial AFC East kings. That day, in turn, began the single-best turnaround in NFL history. The Dolphins went from 1-15 the previous year to 11-5 and division winners in Sparano's first season. They lost a playoff game against Baltimore — the only Dolphins playoff game over a decade stretch. The future looked bright, but never reached those heights again. Ultimately, Sparano's reign suffered like his predecessor's from a lack of a playmaking quarterback, but an added element came when new owner Steve Ross and General Manager Jeff Ireland flew cross-country in a failed attempt to hire Stanford coach Jim Harbaugh. When that news went public, Sparano's relationship with Ireland collapsed and caused strained relations entering the 2011 season. After starting that year with seven straight losses, Sparano was eventually fired during the season. Todd Bowles was named interim coach for the final three games.

{COACH: 2012-PRESENT // RECORD: 23-25}

JOE PHILBIN

Philbin had never been a head coach at any level when Steve Ross hired him before the 2012 season. Such inexperience showed throughout his first three seasons. In his second year, the Dolphins had the most embarrassing chapter in their franchise history when Jonathan Martin left the team's facilities and soon checked into a therapeutic center. That was the start of "Bullygate," in which Richie Incognito, who was battling a personality disorder of his own, was found to have sent troubling messages to Martin. Owner Ross brought in an NFL investigator, and by the end of the fallout, four offensive linemen were replaced, offensive line coach Jim Turner and trainer Kevin O'Neill were fired and Philbin was criticized for not controlling his locker room by NFL coaching legends from Tony Dungy to Jimmy Johnson. That 2013 season was lost completely when the Dolphins dropped the final two games of the year and missed the playoffs. Philbin still was learning how to coach and to talk in 2014, when he admitted to feeling "queasy" about playing aggressively at the end of a game that Green Bay won in the final seconds. The Dolphins finished 8-8, missing the playoffs for Philbin's third straight year, but he was brought back for the 2015 season.

Dolphins logo
2013-present

5
ON THE FIELD

TOP
PLAYS
IN DOLPHINS
HISTORY

**A FAKE SPIKE. A 'LUCKY' RICOCHET. A WILDCAT SCORE.
THESE PLAYS HAVE BECOME LEGENDARY IN MIAMI LORE.**
BY DAVE HYDE

JANUARY 2, 1982
// VS. SAN DIEGO

THE HOOK-AND-LATERAL

Down 24-0, the Dolphins clawed back to 24-10 and then electrified the Orange Bowl crowd on the final play of the first half with a play Tony Nathan said, "never worked in practice." Duriel Harris ran a 15-yard in-route – the "hook" – and caught a pass from Don Strock. Nathan timed a run behind Harris, who lateraled the ball to him. Nathan ran 25 yards into the end zone. San Diego ended up winning the game in overtime, but "hook-and-lateral" endured in Miami Dolphins lore.

NOVEMBER 27, 1994 // AT N.Y. JETS

{2} Dan Marino's "Clock Play" in 1994. "Use it now! Go for the rookie!" Bernie Kosar yelled into the radio in Dan Marino's helmet. Less than 30 seconds left. And ticking. The Dolphins rushed to the line of scrimmage and acted as if Marino would spike the ball. The linemen stood. Marino then threw to Mark Ingram (82), who was covered by rookie Aaron Glenn. Perfect throw. Perfect catch. Perfect play.

DECEMBER 25, 1971 // AT KANSAS CITY

{3} Garo Yepremian's 37-yard field goal ends "The Longest Game" in the 1971 playoffs. As Yepremian ran on the field, Larry Csonka passed him coming off it. "If you miss it, I'll kill you," Csonka said. After Yepremian kicked it, he thought it was good and, as was his habit, turned his back on the ball and jogged to midfield. But the stadium was silent. He panicked. "Did I miss?" he thought. He then realized it was the Kansas City crowd that was silent for the made field goal.

SEPTEMBER 2, 1966 // VS. OAKLAND

{4} Joe Auer returns the franchise-opening kickoff 95 yards for a touchdown in 1966. He had a pet tiger and drove a dune buggy, so he appreciated speed. But when Auer ran back the first-ever kickoff for the Dolphins he became aware of someone running nearly step-for-step with him on the sideline. As he crossed the finish line, he looked over. It was actor and part-owner Danny Thomas, who was so excited he chased after Auer.

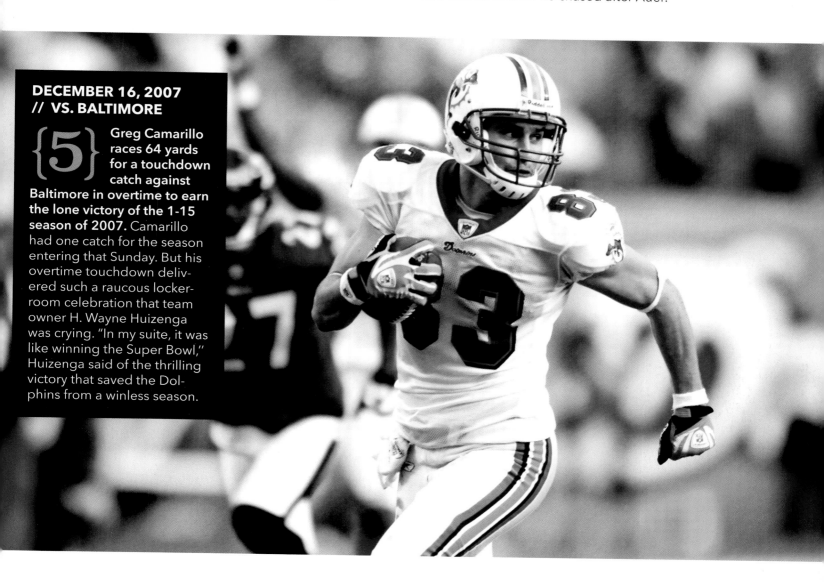

DECEMBER 16, 2007 // VS. BALTIMORE

{5} Greg Camarillo races 64 yards for a touchdown catch against Baltimore in overtime to earn the lone victory of the 1-15 season of 2007. Camarillo had one catch for the season entering that Sunday. But his overtime touchdown delivered such a raucous locker-room celebration that team owner H. Wayne Huizenga was crying. "In my suite, it was like winning the Super Bowl," Huizenga said of the thrilling victory that saved the Dolphins from a winless season.

JANUARY 2, 1972 // VS. BALTIMORE

{6} Dick Anderson's weaving, 62-yard interception return for a touchdown in '71 AFC Championship Game cements the Dolphins' first Super Bowl trip. On Anderson's office wall are time-lapse photos of the run that became of a symbol of that defense's teamwork, as seven blocks were thrown for him. "You're so slow, I went out for a hot dog, came back and you were still running," Dolphins linebacker Nick Buoniconti said.

JANUARY 23, 1983 // VS. N.Y. JETS

{7} A.J. Duhe gets his third interception of the game and returns it 35 yards for a touchdown in the final minutes to ensure a win against the Jets in the 1982 AFC Championship Game. At halftime, it was 0-0 in the Mud Bowl. But in the second half Duhe took over, intercepting three Richard Todd passes, including one to seal the 14-0 win and punch the Dolphins' ticket to the Super Bowl.

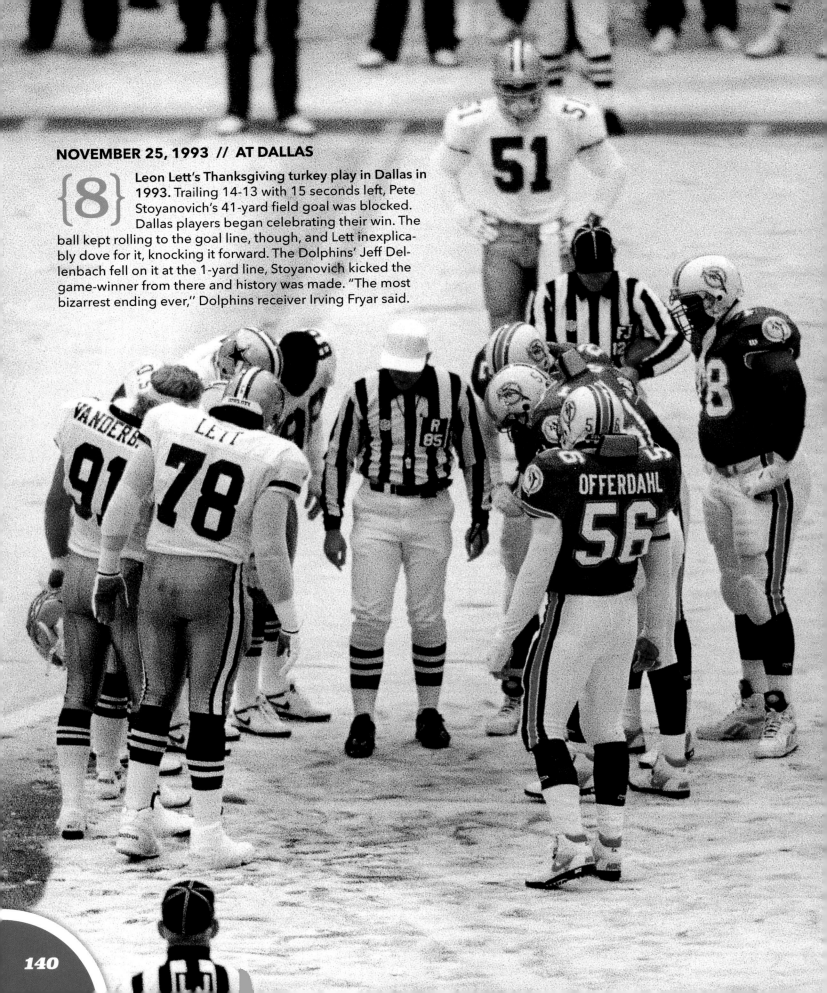

NOVEMBER 25, 1993 // AT DALLAS

{8} Leon Lett's Thanksgiving turkey play in Dallas in 1993. Trailing 14-13 with 15 seconds left, Pete Stoyanovich's 41-yard field goal was blocked. Dallas players began celebrating their win. The ball kept rolling to the goal line, though, and Lett inexplicably dove for it, knocking it forward. The Dolphins' Jeff Dellenbach fell on it at the 1-yard line, Stoyanovich kicked the game-winner from there and history was made. "The most bizarrest ending ever," Dolphins receiver Irving Fryar said.

JANUARY 2, 1999 // VS. BUFFALO

{9} With 17 seconds left and Buffalo at the Dolphins' 5-yard line, Trace Armstrong sacks quarterback Doug Flutie to win the playoff game. "Who says we can't win a big game?" coach Jimmy Johnson yelled in the locker room, slamming a box of "Flutie Flakes" cereal against a table and sending flakes to the locker room floor.

NOVEMBER 10, 1985 // VS. N.Y. JETS

{10} Mark Duper hauls in a Dan Marino rainbow pass with his fingertips, completing a 50-yard touchdown pass with 41 seconds left to the give the Dolphins a 21-17 win against the Jets. Marino came to the line and saw a Jets defense he hadn't seen all night. Safeties were up closer to take an underneath pass, assuming the Dolphins would get close for a tying field goal. Linebackers were blitzing. And one-on-one coverage on Duper outside. "90 take-off," he yelled out at Duper, the audible for Duper go deep. Duper did. Marino threw it. The Orange Bowl shook.

DECEMBER 30, 2000 // VS. INDIANAPOLIS

{11} Lamar Smith's 17-yard touchdown run beats the Colts in overtime in the 2000 playoffs. When the run was over, when he completed his then-franchise records of 40 carries and 209 yards, Lamar Smith had a simple request for teammates piling on him. "I need some air," he said at the bottom of the pile.

DECEMBER 31, 1972 // AT PITTSBURGH

{12}

Larry Seiple runs 37 yards on a fake punt to change the 1972 AFC Championship Game in Pittsburgh and keep the 1972 Perfect Season going. His knee was in such bad shape it was numbed with drugs, but when Seiple saw Pittsburgh's punt-return team turn and run back to block in the fourth quarter, he didn't hesitate. This was seen on film that week. Seiple took off running to the Steelers' 12-yard line. That led to the game-tying touchdown in the eventual win.

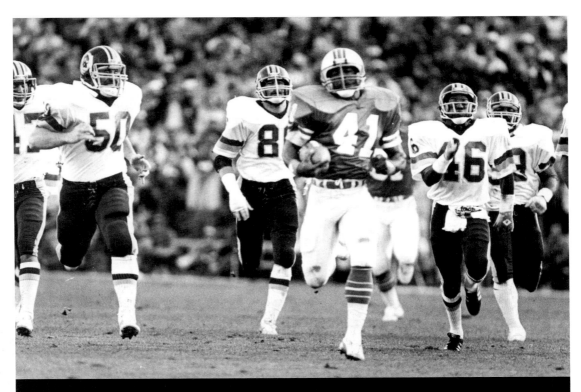

JANUARY 30, 1983 // VS. WASHINGTON

{13}

Fulton Walker returns a kickoff 98 yards for a touchdown, giving the Dolphins a brief 17-10 lead over Washington in the 1983 Super Bowl. Flipping through a game program in his hotel room the night before the game, Walker was surprised to see no kickoffs were returned for a touchdown in the first 16 Super Bowls. "I was always good about saying my prayers at night," he later said. "That night I prayed, 'Please, God, let me be the first guy to run one all the way back.'" Prayer answered.

SEPTEMBER 21, 2008 // AT NEW ENGLAND

{14}

Out of the Wildcat formation unveiled in this game, running back Ronnie Brown throws a 19-yard touchdown to Anthony Fasano in a 2008 upset of New England. With an 0-2 start, Tony Sparano huddled with coaches on the way back from a loss to Arizona. "We've got to do something," he said. Thus, the Wildcat was introduced to the NFL, highlighted by Brown's touchdown throw to Fasano.

SEPTEMBER 4, 1994 // VS. NEW ENGLAND

{16} Dan Marino's 35-yard touchdown pass on fourth down gives the Dolphins a victory over New England in the 1994 season opener. Marino came to the line having been told to get the 5 yards for a first down. His eyes lit up when he saw Irving Fryar in one-on-one coverage outside. He nodded to Fryar, who understood well enough to go for the winning touchdown. "I feel pretty good about what I did," Marino said of the decision.

DECEMBER 3, 1973 // VS. PITTSBURGH

{15}

An intentional safety moves the score from 30-24 to 30-26 in the waning moments, preserving a Monday Night Football win over Steelers. When punter George Roberts began running out of the end zone, Howard Cosell said, "What is he doing?" After some confusion, he did the math on the air. He ended up calling coach Don Shula "a genius."

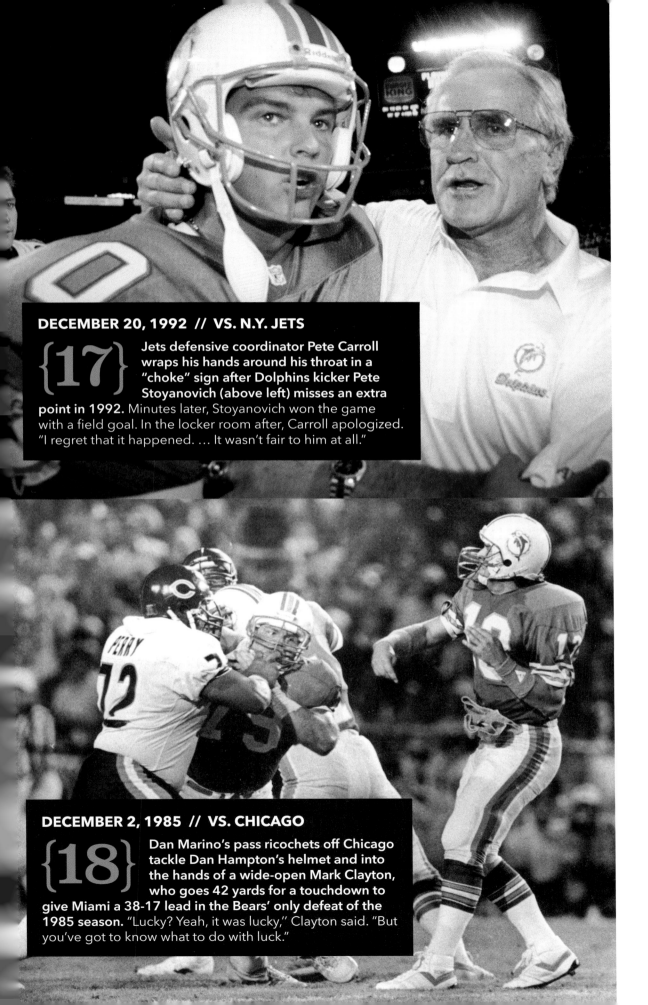

{19}

Cincinnati LB Alex Gordon blind-sides Pete Stoya-novich on a kick-off and then goes laughing to the sideline. Dolphins linebacker Bryan Cox went running into the Bengals sideline, looking for Gordon, taking on any Bengal. The suddenly charged-up Dol-phins went on to romp over Cincin-nati, 37-13.

SEPTEMBER 14, 1980 // VS. CINCINNATI

{20}

The onside punt in 1980. Down 16-7 to Cincinnati, hav-ing just suffered a safety, Don Shula had punter George Roberts skid the ball the requisite 10 yards to make it a live ball. The Dolphins recovered, drove for a touchdown and then added a late field goal to win.

DECEMBER 20, 1992 // VS. N.Y. JETS

{17} Jets defensive coordinator Pete Carroll wraps his hands around his throat in a "choke" sign after Dolphins kicker Pete Stoyanovich (above left) misses an extra point in 1992. Minutes later, Stoyanovich won the game with a field goal. In the locker room after, Carroll apologized. "I regret that it happened. … It wasn't fair to him at all."

DECEMBER 2, 1985 // VS. CHICAGO

{18} Dan Marino's pass ricochets off Chicago tackle Dan Hampton's helmet and into the hands of a wide-open Mark Clayton, who goes 42 yards for a touchdown to give Miami a 38-17 lead in the Bears' only defeat of the 1985 season. "Lucky? Yeah, it was lucky," Clayton said. "But you've got to know what to do with luck."

TOP BLUN-DERS

There has been glory. There has been greatness. However, no one gets to 50 without a few embarrassing missteps.
BY DAVE HYDE AND KEVEN LERNER

IN DOLPHINS HISTORY

{1} RICHIE INCOGNITO-JONATHAN MARTIN BULLYING FIASCO

In 144 embarrassing pages, NFL investigator Ted Wells pulled back the curtains on the Dolphins' 2013 locker room to show a workplace dripping with racially charged language and offensive behavior. Guard Richie Incognito (far left) was labeled the prime offender for his dealings with Jonathan Martin (71). But the repercussions were felt at the top with questions for coach Joe Philbin and owner Steve Ross. The fallout included firing offensive line coach Jim Turner, a lawsuit brought by fired trainer Kevin O'Neill and having to replace four starting linemen the following season. The proud Dolphins brand was dragged through the national mud in a manner no team ever had been.

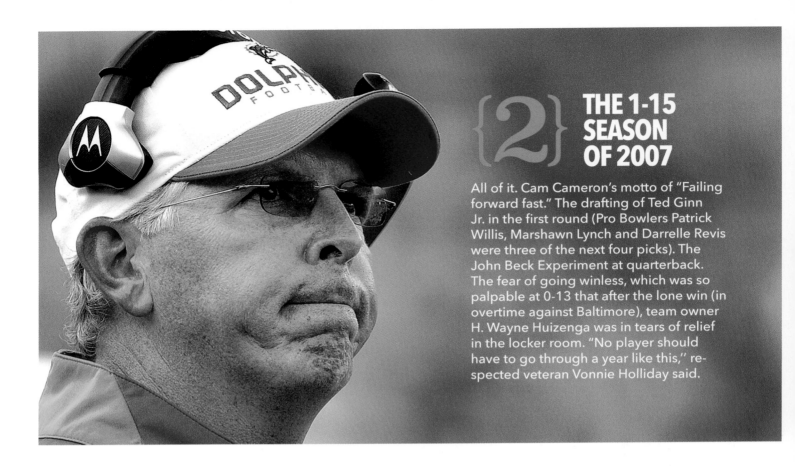

{2} THE 1-15 SEASON OF 2007

All of it. Cam Cameron's motto of "Failing forward fast." The drafting of Ted Ginn Jr. in the first round (Pro Bowlers Patrick Willis, Marshawn Lynch and Darrelle Revis were three of the next four picks). The John Beck Experiment at quarterback. The fear of going winless, which was so palpable at 0-13 that after the lone win (in overtime against Baltimore), team owner H. Wayne Huizenga was in tears of relief in the locker room. "No player should have to go through a year like this," respected veteran Vonnie Holliday said.

{3} CSONKA, TWO OTHERS DEFECT TO THE WFL

The Dolphins had won consecutive Super Bowls and been to three in a row when Larry Csonka (above left), Paul Warfield (not shown) and Jim Kiick (right) signed onto the upstart World Football League before the 1974 season (they played that final season with the Dolphins). "The deal that astonished the sports world," Time magazine called the deal for which Csonka made $1.4 million, Warfield got $900,000 and Kiick earned $700,000. Shula considered it something else — the end of an era.

{4} COURTING OF COACH JIM HARBAUGH

In his first major move, owner Steve Ross took General Manager Jeff Ireland on a cross-country trip to hire Stanford coach Jim Harbaugh. The hiring never happened. Worse, the story broke nationally, and the fallout kept falling through the 2011 season as evidenced by the splintered relationship between Ireland and coach Tony Sparano, who thought he was betrayed. Sparano was fired with three games left in the 2011 season. Harbaugh led the 49ers to a 49-22-1 record the next four years, reaching the NFC title game three times, as well as Super Bowl XLVII.

{5} NICK SABAN'S DEPARTURE IN 2007

One week the Dolphins coach was saying, "I'm not going to be the Alabama coach," the next week he wasn't taking questions on the subject and the following one he was being named the Alabama coach. It proved to be the best move for Saban, who re-established himself as a great college coach. His severe personality wasn't making him friends before this, but combined with the unfortunate way he left the team, it was one of the uglier chapters in Dolphins history.

DOLPHINS   JAGUARS
    7   62
DOWN   TO GO   BALL ON   QTR
 3   5   44   4

{6} JAGUARS 62, DOLPHINS 7 (JAN. 15, 2000)

It was a second-round playoff game and that should protect it from some ugly thoughts. But it being the worst loss in team history and the ending statement of the great careers of quarterback Dan Marino and coach Jimmy Johnson make it an unfortunate day to remember.

{7} THE FEUD BETWEEN ROBBIE AND SHULA GOES PUBLIC

Robbie's best move as owner was hiring coach Shula, but in time, the two strong personalities clashed. It went public at a Fontainebleau Hotel banquet celebrating their second Super Bowl title. Shula was waiting outside, and Robbie was badgering him to come in. "Yell at me again, and I'll knock you on your ass," Shula said. They bickered over who would talk last. Robbie quit taking Shula's calls. Since both were Catholics, the Archbishop of Miami was asked to intervene. The next day, the Miami News headline read: "The Exorcist: Archbishop ousts devil in Dolphins leaders."

{8} MISSING ON STAR QB DREW BREES – TWICE

The day before the 2001 draft, Dolphins director of college scouting Tom Braatz entered coach Dave Wannstedt's office and pleaded with him one final time to draft Brees with the No. 26 pick. Wannstedt said they would take cornerback Jamar Fletcher. Five years later, Nick Saban had a choice to make: Brees or Daunte Culpepper. To be fair, Brees wasn't an instant success, and Saban's decision involved delicate medical issues. But twice in five years the Dolphins could have had the kind of franchise quarterback who would have spared the team a lot of pain.

{9} RICKY WILLIAMS' ODYSSEY

You could file Ricky Williams under a success story considering he eventually worked himself back into good graces. But his quitting the team a few days before the 2004 training camp to live in a tent in Australia was a prime reason that season failed and a regime change was made. He returned a year later, only to be suspended for the 2006 season for testing positive for marijuana.

{10} THE JOE PHILBIN-JEFF IRELAND RELATIONSHIP

The relationship between the Dolphins coach and general manager soured so completely during the 2013 season that they didn't even speak to each other. Underlings were forced to choose sides to survive. Executive vice president of football Dawn Aponte sided with Philbin. So did owner Steve Ross. Philbin returned. Ireland was fired. Another season suffered from the non-working relationship.

151

HOME FIELD

The Dolphins played their franchise opener in the Orange Bowl in 1966 and stayed there through the 1986 season. Around 1980, Dolphins owner Joe Robbie began lobbying for a new stadium. Local politicians refused for years, so Robbie built one with his own money. In 1987, Joe Robbie Stadium opened in what is now Miami Gardens.

BY MARK DUPER
{ DOLPHINS WIDE RECEIVER // 1982-92 }

They were opposite homes in every way. The Orange Bowl was a feeling in your gut. Joe Robbie Stadium was an idea in your head. The Orange Bowl was so old the lockers had one hook to hang your clothes. Joe Robbie Stadium was so new you could eat off the locker room floor.

Duper

If there's one difference, it's that Joe Robbie Stadium was a beautiful place to watch a football game, and the Orange Bowl was an unmatched place to have a football game. The crowd was right on top of you in the Orange Bowl, the noise running through you like an electric current. Maybe it was my age. Maybe it was because I didn't play in large stadiums in college at Northwestern State. But the sound inside the Orange Bowl was like nothing I ever heard again in my life.

Here's what it was like, in one play: We trailed the Jets, 17-14, in the final minutes in 1985. I came to the line, looked across at the single cover for me and looked at Dan Marino. He saw the same thing I did. I ran deep. Marino threw long. I stretched out my hand as far as it would go, reaching for the ball, and just tipped it enough to pat it in the air in front of me. The stadium was silent. But as I grabbed the ball and I ran in with the winning touchdown, it sounded like New Year's Eve inside my helmet in a way no place ever could.

Leaving the Orange Bowl for Joe Robbie Stadium was like trading a Volkswagen for a Cadillac. Joe Robbie had a dream and he made it come true with that stadium. There was none better in football. Everything was first-class inside it. Every player appreciated the new home we had. Sure, it was different, and so it took a while for everyone to grow accustomed to playing there. But who wouldn't enjoy a new home?

The way I explain it, I got the best of the old world and the best of the new world in my career. There was no better traditional stadium than the Orange Bowl. And there was no more modern stadium than Joe Robbie Stadium.

{ AS TOLD TO DAVE HYDE }

152

ORANGE BOWL
1966-86

JOE ROBBIE STADIUM
1987-present (now SunLife Stadium)

153

WHAT'S IN A NAME?

Since the Dolphins left the Orange Bowl they have played at the same stadium, which was originally named for the team's first owner and the driving force behind the stadium, Joe Robbie.

Although the location in Miami-Dade County, just south of the Broward County line, has stayed the same, the name of the stadium has changed many times over the years.

Aug. 16, 1987-Aug. 25, 1996	Joe Robbie Stadium
Aug. 26, 1996-Sept. 9, 1996	Pro Player Park
Sept. 10, 1996-Jan. 9, 2005	Pro Player Stadium
Jan. 10, 2005-April 7, 2006	Dolphins Stadium
April 8, 2006-May 7, 2009	Dolphin Stadium
May 8, 2009-Jan. 5, 2010	Land Shark Stadium
Jan. 6, 2010-Jan. 19, 2010	Dolphin Stadium
Jan. 20, 2010-present	**Sun Life Stadium**

The Orange Bowl, scene of so much Dolphins success, was torn down in 2008. At right, Joe Robbie Stadium rises above the neighborhood in 1986. At far right, a look inside Joe Robbie Stadium in 1986 and, next page, under the lights in its first year. ▶

THE FANS

Whether it's exulting through years of supremacy and setting records, or enduring another disappointing season and head-shaking draft decisions, Miami Dolphins fans are the most loyal, plentiful and vocal on the South Florida sports landscape. They eagerly suffer through stifling humidity and heat, scorching sun or pouring rain to support their team. They flood talk radio with criticism, advice and excitement — year round. They wear, paint — and they will insist, bleed — aqua and orange.

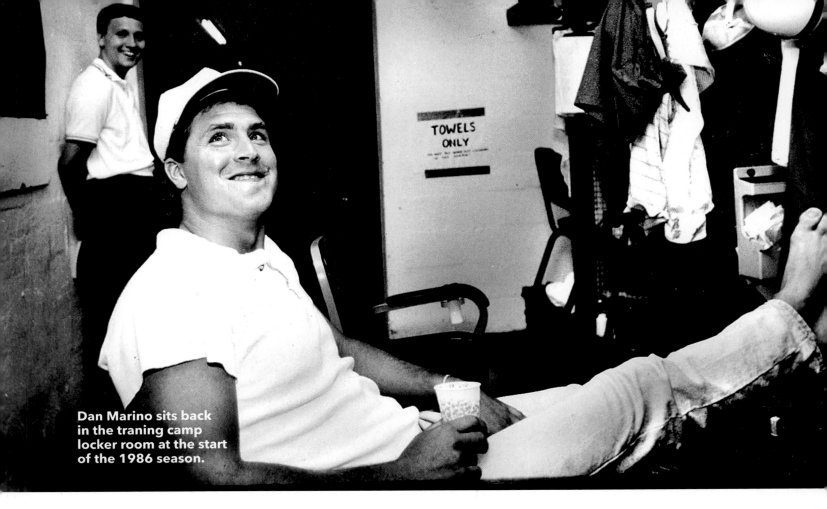

Dan Marino sits back in the traning camp locker room at the start of the 1986 season.

PHOTOGRAPHY CREDITS

Sun Sentinel staff

p.3: Ursula Seemann
p.5: Joe Amon
p.8: Andrew Innerarity
p.11, Robbie: Eliot Schechter
p.11, Huizenga: Robert Duyos
p.11, Ross: Robert Duyos
p.15: Robert Duyos
p.16: Lou Toman
p.17: Donn Gould
p.19, bottom: Donn Gould
p.19, top: Donn Gould
p.20, bottom: Sun Sentinel file
p.20, top: Sun Sentinel file
p.21: Lou Toman
p.22: Ursula Seemann
p.24: Andrew Innerarity
p.25: Ursula Seemann
p.26: Sun Sentinel file
p.28: Bill Bates
p.29: Ursula Seemann
p.30: Bob East III
p.32: Nicholas R. Von Staden
p.33: Nicholas R. Von Staden
p.34: Bob East III
p.37, bottom: Deborah Meeks
p.37, top: Robert Mayer
p.39: Robert Mayer
p.41: Robert Mayer
p.42: Bob Mack
p.43, bottom: Sun Sentinel file
p.43, top: Bob Mack
p.44: Jill Guttman
p.46: Sun Sentinel file
p.50: Lou Toman

p.51: Robert Duyos
p.52: Ursula Seemann
p.54: Ursula Seemann
p.56: Robert Duyos
p.58, bottom: Robert Duyos
p.58, top: Robert Duyos
p.59, bottom: Robert Duyos
p.59, top: Robert Duyos
p.60: Jim Rassol
p.61: Jim Rassol
p.62, bottom: Robert Duyos
p.62, top: Jim Rassol
p.63: Robert Duyos
p.64: Andrew Innerarity
p.65: Robert Duyos
p.67: Robert Duyos
p.68: Robert Duyos
p.70: Robert Duyos
p.72: Robert Duyos
p.74: Jim Rassol
p.75: Mike Stocker
p.79, Marino: Robert Mayer
p.80, Csonka: Charles Trainor Jr.
p.80, Little: Sun Sentinel file
p.80, Stephenson: Robert Duyos
p.81, Buoniconti: Sun Sentinel file
p.81, Griese: Bill Bates
p.81, Langer: Sun Sentinel file
p.81, Taylor: Robert Duyos
p.81, Warfield: Ursula Seemann
p.82, Baumhower: Robert Mayer
p.82, Clayton: Eliot J. Schechter
p.82, Kuechenberg: Ursula Seemann
p.82, Thomas: Andrew Innerarity
p.83, Anderson: Ursula Seemann
p.83, Betters: Sun Sentinel file
p.83, Offerdahl: Eliot J. Schechter
p.83, Scott: Ursula Seemann
p.83, Stanfill: Donn Gould
p.83, Webb: John Curry
p.84, Cox: Robert Duyos

p.84, Duper: Robert Mayer
p.84, Fernandez: Lou Toman
p.84, Kiick: Arnold Ernest
p.84, Moore: Ursula Seemann
p.85, Madison: Preston C. Mack
p.85, McDuffie: Robert Duyos
p.85, Morris: Pam Bates
p.85, Newman: Bill Sanders
p.85, Surtain: Robert Duyos
p.86, Matheson: Bob Matheson
p.86, Wake: Joe Cavaretta
p.86, Nathan: Keith Hadley
p.86, Roby: Nicholas Von Staden
p.86, Yepremian: A. Enrique Valentin
p.87, Bokamper: Les Sintay
p.87, Bowens: Nicholas Von Staden
p.87, Brudzinski: Susan Stocker
p.87, Cross: John Curry
p.87, Giesler: Ed Wagner Jr.
p.87, den Herder: Sun Sentinel file
p.88, Hardy: Sun Sentinel file
p.88, Jensen: Bob Mack
p.88, Mare: Robert Duyos
p.88, Sims: Eliot J. Schechter
p.88, Williams: Robert Duyos
p.89, Dellenbach: Robert Duyos
p.89, Mandich: Sun Sentinel file
p.89, Pennington: Robert Duyos
p.89, Ruddy: Michael Laughlin
p.89: Robert Duyos
p.90: Don Gould
p.93: Robert Duyos
p.94: Bob Mack
p.97: Robert Mayer
p.105, Fletcher: Robert Duyos
p.105, Jordan: Robert Duyos
p.105, Marino: Robert Azmitia
p.105, Stephenson: Ursula Seemann
p.106, Avery: Robert Duyos
p.106, Csonka: Lou Toman
p.106, Griese: Sun Sentinel file

p.106, Kumerow: Anne Ryan
p.107, Green: Preston C. Mack
p.107, Smith: Robert Duyos
p.107, Taylor: Robert Duyos
p.107, Thomas: Robert Duyos
p.108, Allen: Robert Duyos
p.108, Cox: John Curry
p.108, Ginn: Rhonda Vanover
p.108, Scott: Ursula Seemann
p.109, Clayton: Robert Mayer
p.109, Milner: Robert Mayer
p.109, Shipp: Robert Mayer
p.109, Webb: Ursula Seemann
p.110: Robert Duyos
p.111: Andrew Innerarity
p.112: Robert Duyos
p.114: Arnold Ernest
p.115: Bob East III
p.116: Lou Toman
p.117: Bill Bates
p.118: Lou Toman
p.119: Andrew Innerarity
p.120: Ron Kenney
p.121: Sun Sentinel file
p.122: Robert Duyos
p.123: Robert Duyos
p.126, left: Lou Toman
p.126, right: John Curry
p.127: Andrew Innerarity
p.128: Sun Sentinel file
p.129: Robert Duyos
p.130: Robert Duyos
p.131, Cameron: Robert Duyos
p.131, Saban: Joe Amon
p.132: Robert Duyos
p.133: Robert Duyos
p.136: Robert Mayer
p.138: John Curry
p.139: Joe Amon
p.141: Robert Mayer
p.142, top right and left: Jim Rassol

p.142, bottom: Robert Duyos
p.143, top: Con Keyes
p.143, bottom: Jim Rassol
p.144: Sun Sentinel file
p.145, top: Eliot Schechter
p.147, bottom left: Jim Rassol
p.147, bottom right: Jim Rassol
p.147, top left: Carline Jean
p.147, top right: Joe Cavaretta
p.148, bottom right: Joe Cavaretta
p.148, bottom left: Ursula Seemann
p.148, top: Robert Duyos
p.149: Robert Duyos
p.150, bottom: Robert Duyos
p.150, top: Preston C. Mack
p.151, bottom left: Lou Toman
p.151, bottom right: Robert Duyos
p.151, top left: John Curry
p.151, top right: Jim Rassol
p.153, Joe Robbie: Carl Seibert
p.153, Orange Bowl: Omar Vega
p.155, left: Eliot J. Schechter
p.155, right: Robert Mayer
p.155, top: Robert Duyos
p.156: Carl Seibert
p.158, fan photos: Sun Sentinel staff
p.159: Robert Duyos
p.160: Robert Mayer

Other sources

p.26, bottom left: Mark Foley, AP
p.36: Larry Sharkey, Los Angeles Times
p.49: Amy Sancetta, AP
p.89, Foley: AP file
p.113: AP file
p.126, middle: George Rose, Los Angeles Times
p.140: Glenn James, AP
p.145, bottom: Ed Wagner Jr., Chicago Tribune